D1596799

LENIN AND THE
CULTURAL REVOLUTION

MARXIST THEORY AND CONTEMPORARY CAPITALISM

General Editor: John Mepham

This is a new series of texts, of new British books and of translations committed to:
the development of Marxist theory
the analysis of contemporary capitalism, its tendencies and contradictions
the record of struggles to which they give rise.

Also in this series:

Charles Bettelheim
The Transition to Socialist Economy

Michel Bosquet
Capitalism in Crisis and Everyday Life

Claudie Broyelle
Women's Liberation in China

Colin Henfrey and Bernardo Sorj (eds.)
Chilean Voices: Activists describe their
Experiences of the Popular Unity Period

David-Hillel Ruben
Marxism and Materialism: A Study in Marxist
Theory of Knowledge

Lucien Sève
Man in Marxist Theory and the Psychology
of Personality

Dave Laing
The Marxist Theory of Art

André Gorz (ed.)
The Division of Labour: The Labour
Process and Class Struggle in Modern Capitalism

Tom Clarke and Laurie Clements
Trades Unions under Capitalism

LENIN
AND THE
CULTURAL
REVOLUTION

CARMEN CLAUDIN-URONDO

TRANSLATED FROM THE FRENCH BY
BRIAN PEARCE

THE HARVESTER PRESS · SUSSEX
HUMANITIES PRESS · NEW JERSEY

First published in Britain by
THE HARVESTER PRESS LIMITED
2 Stanford Terrace, Hassocks, Sussex
Publisher: John Spiers

and in the USA by
HUMANITIES PRESS INC.,
Atlantic Highlands, New Jersey 07716

© The Harvester Press Limited, 1977

First published in France as *lénine et la
révolution culturelle*, by Mouton et Cie, 1975

Translated from the French by Brian Pearce

British Library Cataloguing in Publication Data

Claudin-Urondo, Carmen
  Lenin and the cultural revolution. — (Marxist theory
  and contemporary capitalism).
  1. Russia — History — 1917- 2. Russia — Politics and
  government — 1917-1936 3. Russia — Civilization —
  1917-
  I. Title II. Pearce, Brian, b. 1915 III. Series
  947.084'1   DK265

  ISBN 0-85527-800-5

Humanities Press Inc.
ISBN 0-391-00739-4

Photoset by Red Lion Setters, Holborn, London,
and printed by Redwood Burn Ltd., Trowbridge and Esher

Contents

INTRODUCTION: PROLETARIAN REVOLUTION
AND CULTURAL REVOLUTION

Part One

THE DOMINANT POINT OF VIEW

Part Two

WHAT DOMINATES THIS POINT OF VIEW

Introduction

PROLETARIAN REVOLUTION AND CULTURAL REVOLUTION

The aim of the proletarian revolution, as defined by its first theoreticians, is to give the proletariat, and thereby society as a whole, the power to free itself from "the reign of necessity" and to build "the reign of freedom", classless society, on the basis of the abolition of all forms of exploitation of man by man. Though very summary, this outline immediately inspires at least two developments which are directly connected with the theme to be analysed.

While the taking of political power by the proletariat marks the moment in time when the break is made between the two "reigns", the transition from one to the other itself takes place over a period which cannot be determined in advance. It is a process in which retreats, whether merely tactical or objectively necessary, are not out of the question, and the very nature of which consists precisely in the antagonistic co-existence of elements derived from both the old and the new social orders. The taking of political power nevertheless signifies a decisive step, which gives sanction to the protracted progress of this upheaval — compared by Engels to the upheavals in Nature. It is in relation to the taking of power that the "pre-revolutionary" and the "post-revolutionary" are articulated. However, just as the revolution did not begin with this political overthrow, neither does it end with it: the revolution continues, but now on a basis which is already radically different. Nothing is, or can be, like it was before. In order to become irreversible, the break must be radical and total.

The desire and the need to change completely the previous social system leads to the second development. In order to accomplish its purpose and bring about a society that will be transparent to itself, the revolution must affect, at every level, all spheres of human activity, all the relations men have established among themselves and with the world. The revolution's first liberating act takes place in that source where the opaque and overwhelming veil of man's social alienation is spun, namely, its material, economic basis, the keystone of which is production-relations. Changing, or, more precisely, starting to change, from the very outset, this cornerstone of the economic system is the condition *sine qua non*, equivalent to a categorical imperative, that determines the whole range of possibilities for the future existence of a new world that will at last be truly human. But the task remains to be completed. In the social edifice of which it is the foundation, the economic factor, though determining, is so only "ultimately", being imbricated in the complex action and reaction of all the elements that make up the political, legal and social superstructure, "in which, amid all the endless host of accidents ..., the economic movement finally asserts itself as necessary."[1] It is the relations established, on the basis of the necessary overturn in the economic order, between that order and all the crucial spheres of the superstructure, that condition the outcome of the revolution.

As they emerge, indeed, from this "endless host of accidents", the new economic movement, and consequently the new society that it engenders, will undoubtedly be different from the system that has been abolished; but they may nevertheless prove alien to the purpose that was aimed at, namely, classless society. Thus, as we shall see in the case of the Russian Revolution, and in the determined sphere of the cultural revolution, the revolutionary project may miscarry, giving birth to a child which is deformed, distorted in comparison with the purpose proclaimed, but of which all the same, it is indeed the father. Likewise, the designated subject of the revolutionary task, the proletariat, not only fails to carry out its historical mission of freeing society from class domination by freeing itself, but it is in its name, unfailingly invoked by a mystifying official liturgy, that the new ruling power justifies its own existence and legitimises a domination the first victims of which are, inevitably, the proletariat itself, enchained as soon as elevated to sanctity, and the aims of the revolution, derailed as soon as turned into fetishes. Exploitation, and therefore alienation, silently sets up its throne again, with only, after all, a difference of form.

It is impossible, within the limits of the present study, to give an exhaustive analysis of the many reasons for this phenomenon of "distortion", which there is cause to believe was only *potentially* present at the beginning of the Russian Revolution. Hard to foresee, even though Marx and Engels did have a certain premonition of it,[2] this phenomenon, which has not been sufficiently clarified, calls for investigation, by every Marxist especially — an investigation which would benefit from being carried out as collective and multidisciplinary research. In any case, it is in the framework of the problematic of this many-faceted distortion that I propose to single out and analyse, and thereby criticise, one of its most essential manifestations (which is also, perhaps, one of the least-known), namely, the cultural revolution. The evident resonance of this idea, the topicality of which shows what a real problem it reflects, is nowadays associated almost exclusively with the recent experience of Maoism. It can be said at once that the conception of the cultural revolution in China, embracing the general revolutionary process with which it is identified, possesses, as I shall try to show, a much wider significance than it had in the country of the first proletarian revolution, and, especially, for Lenin himself. The topicality of the Chinese cultural revolution makes reference to it obligatory, but such reference as is made (mainly for purposes of comparison) will be subordinate in my analysis to the Russian Revolution and the conception of the cultural revolution that we find in Lenin's thought.

The methodological procedure I have chosen will consist, in fact, of approaching the subject under consideration by localising it, in the strict sense of the term, that is, by examining it in the actual place where it appeared concretely — the first, if not the promised, land of its real history. The choice of this procedure is due to a desire not to attempt an abstract reflexion on the problematic of the cultural revolution, but instead to analyse how this was grasped and theorised about at the moment when it became, for the proletarian revolution in Russia, a concrete reality and an experienced problematic. However, my analysis makes no claim to be exhaustive. It will deal, as the title indicates, essentially with the thought of Lenin, who formed a theory of the cultural revolution that resulted from his reflexion upon the revolutionary experience. Two reasons, one concerned with method and the other with history, decided my choice. On the one hand, it seemed to me more fruitful, as regards both the clarity and the depth of the analysis, to focus this upon a body of thought; and, on the other, the selection of this particular body of thought is explained by its importance, which needs no proof, in the history of the revolutionary movement.

What I am going to do, then, is to examine the actual writings of the Russian Revolution, and in particular those of Lenin, what they say and what they are silent about, their relation to reality as it was conceived and to the aims that were proclaimed — so as, in short, to discover how these ideas affected the fate of the first proletarian revolution.

NOTES

1 Engels, letter to Josef Bloch, 21 September, 1890: *Selected Correspondence*, Moscow, F.L.P.H., 1956, p.498.

2 "The worst thing that can befall a leader of an extreme party is to be compelled to take over a government in an epoch when the movement is not yet ripe for the domination of the class which he represents, and for the realisation of the measures which that domination implies ... Thus, he necessarily finds himself in an unsolvable dilemma. What he *can* do contradicts all his previous actions, principles and immediate interests of his party, and what he *ought* to do cannot be done. In a word, he is compelled to represent not his party or his class, but the class for whose domination the movement is then ripe. In the interests of the movement he is compelled to advance the interests of an alien class, and to feed his own class with phrases and promises, and with the asseveration that the interests of that alien class are their own interests. Whoever is put into this awkward position is irrevocably lost." (Engels, *The Peasant War*, Moscow, F.L.P.H., 1956, pp.138, 139.)

Part One

THE DOMINANT POINT OF VIEW

I. THE PROBLEMATIC OF THE CULTURAL REVOLUTION

The fundamental texts dealing with the problems of the cultural revolution mostly date from the decisive period of the 1920s. They testify, by their existence and their very diversity, to the richness of life and creative potentialities of a period which, with all its contradictions, provides the example of a cultural revolution coming to birth — that richness which meant, precisely, that it gave nourishment both to what could help the cultural revolution live *and* to what could cause it to miscarry. These texts bear, moreover, the marks of originality, both theoretical (the revolution had not broken out first of all in the place where "it should have") and practical (confronted with facts, the theoreticians were called upon to reply, there and then, to "unforeseen" questions). Lenin testified to this when he said, forthrightly, in characterising the "extraordinary" phenomenon of the Russian Revolution: "Napoleon, I think, wrote : '*On s'engage et puis ...on voit.*' Rendered freely, this means: 'First engage in a serious battle and then see what happens. Well, we did..."[1]

I am going to try to show, from what happened after that, why and how the problem of the cultural revolution, of its relation to the political and economic revolution, emerged as one of the most, if not *the* most, "determining" of problems.

It was mentioned earlier that the taking of political

power actually meant the opening of the gate for revolution, that is, for that period of transition the characteristic feature of which is, precisely, the "revolutionising" of production-relations and of social relations at all levels. In a sense, the notions of cultural revolution, political revolution, economic revolution, are abstract working categories. But their abstract character is useful because the conceptual distinction they enable us to make (revolution in the economy, in politics, in culture, and so on) simply grasps, in its inner specificity, without separating it from its various extrinsic determinants, a particular group of social, human phenomena which, in concrete reality, forms one of the constituent parts of a complex structure made up of indissociable elements, each of them geared, directly or otherwise, to the rest. The process is therefore dialectical at every moment, with a dynamic of its own that determines the activity of men (of a class, or a social group), activity which in turn conditions it: it is at one and the same time conditioning and conditioned. Thus, man's independent activity is at once consciousness and knowledge of these (his own) determinations and of his action upon them as a function thereof. His freedom is exercised upon and within the field of possibilities that reality offers. And, as we have seen, to say that economic determination operates, though decisively, only "ultimately", in the last analysis, also means to say that one of these spheres which embrace reality and are identified with it (the political, the economic, or the cultural sphere) can, at a certain moment of the process, assume priority over the others, placing itself on the agenda of a particular phase of history. When this is grasped, conscious activity can be carried on which is deliberately aimed at *that* sphere more than any other. It was in this way that, on the morrow of the October Revolution, when the guns fell silent amid the ruins, the cultural problem, the need for a cultural revolution, presented itself and took shape as *the* problem before the Russian Revolution, while awaiting the world revolution. What was still required was to agree upon the meaning to be ascribed to the concepts of culture and cultural revolution.

While everybody was at one on the nature of culture in the communist society of the future (a culture that would be truly human because freed from any class determination), this was not the case when it came to defining culture — its content and its function in the revolutionary process — in the period of transition, the period which was crucial since the outcome of the revolution was organically bound up with it. What was at issue was deciding the nature of the relations that should exist between the proletarian revolution and culture during this phase when the new society was coming to maturity; and describing it on the basis of the central question which the problematic of the cultural revolution presented as its corollary, namely, the question of proletarian culture. More concretely, what had to be done was to answer a series of questions which fundamentally concerned the very nature of the revolution that was in progress: could one, should one, create a proletarian culture, as an organic expression of the new proletarian order, an antithesis to bourgeois culture? (If the ruling culture was the culture of the ruling class, ought not the proletariat to have its own class culture?) What function should this proletarian culture fulfil, and to what end in the revolutionary process? Finally, what relations (of tolerance, subordination or exclusion) should it maintain with bourgeois culture — which, inherited from capitalism, was still, even though dethroned, dominant in a certain way — and, in particular, with the direct depositories of this culture, the "bourgeois intellectuals"? These questions, which arose at that time, already showed clearly all that required answering, despite the almost complete theoretical silence maintained by Marxist literature on the matters concerned.

It was this entire problematic that Bukharin synthesised after seven years of experience of the revolution: "There is one question in connexion with this, which in my opinion acquires very great importance. This question has still to be developed from the theoretical point of view; it is the question of the *cultural problem* during the transitional period. I think that this is a question on which there are many theses scattered throughout a number of Lenin's works. One must add to these his speech at the Youth Congress, [his statements] concerning the role and use of specialists, and his speech and theses concerning Communist education as well as the question of the combination of so-called proletarian culture with old culture and definite succession in this respect [see note — Trans.]. All these questions combined must also be subjected to theoretical analysis. They also represent one of the most important problems of modern times, and I think that *we may even now say that certain fundamentals in the theoretical conceptions of Vladimir Ilyich may also be found here* [my emphasis, C.C-U.] We must continue this work. This question is again quite new. No one had or could have broached it in the previous phase of historical development. This did not exist with the most revolutionary Marxist or with Marx himself. This is a new task — the task of our future."[2]

This summary of the question as it then stood is particularly interesting because of the indication which it gives us, in passing, of a certain attitude towards Lenin's conceptions. When he says that all these matters have been dealt with already by Lenin, so far as "certain fundamentals" are concerned, Bukharin is only repeating an idea which was already dominant at that time, and which was to become institutionalised in a more and more "sacralising" form — namely, that Lenin's thinking on this question, as on many others, was the obligatory axis of reference, if not the actual solution, for all the problems involved. Bukharin here subscribes unquestioningly to a situation in which it was becoming a ritual to invoke Lenin's name for ever more mystificatory purposes. In short, Lenin's thought was beginning to experience, very quickly, the fate suffered by some revolutionaries of the past, and which he himself had indignantly denounced in *The State and Revolution*: "After their death, attempts are made to convert them into harmless icons, to canonise them, so to say, and to hallow their *names* to a certain extent for the 'consolation' of the oppressed classes and with the object of duping the latter, while at the same time robbing the revolutionary theory of its *substance*, blunting its revolutionary edge and vulgarising it. Today, the bourgeoisie and the opportunists within the labour movement concur in this doctoring of Marxism. They omit, obscure or distort the revolutionary side of this theory, its revolutionary soul."[3]

II. LENIN'S AS THE DOMINANT POINT OF VIEW

A. *The texts*

It is clear that Lenin's line on the problematic of the cultural revolution was not, as we shall see, the only one existing in the 1920s. Nevertheless, it was Lenin's ideas on the matter which (as Bukharin's remark shows, though as yet with some discretion) not only ended by imposing themselves as the point of departure for the subsequent development of official thinking, but were also, from the outset, taken as the axis of reference in the discussion that developed. This is why, as I have already said, it seemed proper to focus this analysis upon Lenin's thought — precisely because it was his point of view that was dominant, and therefore capable, first and foremost, of providing us with the keys to the thought of its epoch.

Some preliminary observations need to be made, since they strike one immediately upon reading for the first time Lenin's principal writings on the subject.

First, these writings are mostly[4] also the ones that are, in general, regarded as fundamental for the expression of Lenin's ideas about the revolution as these ideas matured *after* the capture of power.

Then, all these writings bear very strongly the mark of their author, that is, of a *revolutionary in power*, the man of the Party and of the State who is obliged, from moment to moment, to confront his theory of *the* revolution with the reality of *a* revolution. From this circumstance result sometimes some theoretical "short-cuts, in which a certain pragmatism appears, and sometimes a tendency (a temptation?) to try and make reality fit the schemata of theory.

Finally, these writings are marked by a lack of systematisation of the ideas expressed, which does not mean that they lack coherence. "Everything hangs together", but it is left to the reader to give flesh to the spirit, defining the essential articulations and testing the validity of the assumptions made.

A first reading of Lenin's writings is enough to bring out the great importance he accords to the realisation of the cultural revolution and the historic mission with which he invests it: "In our country the political and social revolution preceded the cultural revolution, that very cultural revolution which nevertheless now confronts us. This cultural revolution would now suffice to make our country a completely socialist country."[5]

It is noteworthy, however, that when this reading has been completed, one finds that the expression "cultural revolution" has figured very rarely in Lenin's vocabulary, whereas the word "culture" has recurred like a leitmotiv, especially in his last works. A fundamental conception, which is nevertheless employed infrequently: this "statistical" observation already points to what will constitute my working hypothesis, namely, that when he proclaims the urgency of the cultural revolution, Lenin's preoccupation, even obsession, where the survival of the revolution is concerned, is not so much the *transformation* of culture as the *acquisition* of the culture inherited from the former ruling class, bourgeois culture. It is therefore by analysing the meaning, or meanings, that Lenin gave to the concept of culture that, it seems to me, we can clarify what he meant by the cultural revolution.

B. *The concept of culture*

The term "culture" has, in Lenin's writings, three main connotations[6]: (i) culture as civilisation, (ii) culture as ideology, (iii) culture as knowledge. To strictly follow the increasing order of importance that Lenin himself assigns to each of these senses, we would need to transpose the first two, "civilisation" and "ideology." However, the order chosen corresponds above all to a concern to bring out the mechanism of Lenin's thinking, in which the problem of the permanence and reinforcement of ideology is always subordinated, once political power is in the hands of the Soviets and the Party, to the problem of the attainment of knowledge and, *thereby*, of civilisation.

Lenin's interest, in fact, is directed much less to the

intrinsic connexion between the three terms than to the particular relation between each of them *and the revolution*. He determines the nature of this relation by reference to *immediate* practical needs, to the current historical moment, in order words, by reference to the reply he gives to the questions: "What presents the greatest danger to our revolution?", "What is the most urgent problem for our revolution?". Lenin's reply is categorical: the gravest danger threatening our revolution is the lack of culture-as-knowledge, and, consequently, the lack of civilisation. Solve that problem, and the revolution will be irreversible. The line of reasoning is a simple one: when we have attained civilisation, the problem of ideology, of the ideological allegiance of the masses, will be solved; and there is only one means to arrive at this end, namely, to "learn" existing knowledge, to "learn" bourgeois culture.

1. CULTURE AS CIVILISATION

Certain passages, then, justify us, in the first place, in relating "culture" to "civilisation", with the latter understood primarily in its broadest sense, as the material and spiritual attainment of a particular type of society at a given moment of its evolution, that is, at a particular level of development of its productive forces. It is this broad sense of the concept "civilisation" that enables Lenin to speak of a certain indestructibility of civilisation, despite the "massive destruction of cultural values and means of production" through which the revolution will have to cut its way, gradually and with difficulty, towards fruition:

> "For no matter to what extent culture has been destroyed, it cannot be removed from history; it will be difficult to restore, but no destruction will ever

mean the complete disappearance of that culture. Some part of it, some material remains of that culture will be indestructible, the difficulties will be only in restoring it."[7]

However, this sense of the term, embracing every type of civilisation without singling out one type as against any other, does usually assume, with Lenin, a precise content, indicating a concrete reality — that which, in his eyes, represents civilisation *par excellence*: the industrial societies of the West.

Basically, indeed, whenever Lenin speaks of civilisation, what he thinks of is, always and exclusively, Western, and more precisely still, European civilisation. It is to this type of civilisation that Russia must aspire if it wants to carry its revolution through to completion, for it is this which, for Lenin, combines all the material (productive and social) conditions without which socialism would remain unachievable. Western civilisation offers Russia a ready-made model to which it can and must conform, and which only needs to be adapted to the political form of the proletarian regime. Here we come upon a major point in Lenin's thinking which we shall meet again and again throughout this analysis, and which it is essential to develop in all its aspects, within the framework of the theme under consideration. What we see here is the distinction which Lenin tends to make — and the mechanistic nature of which I shall try to show — between, in this particular case, capitalism's Western civilisation and capitalist *politics*, without ever getting around to raising explicitly the question of the organic connexions (other than those effected by the dominant bourgeois ideology) that may exist between the two terms. One might say that, for Lenin, this civilisation does not possess the political and social system it deserves, that its true character (wonderful inventions, highly developed technology, etc.) is, so to speak, falsified by the circumstance that it is enslaved by capitalism.[8] It will therefore be enough for the proletarian regime to take it over for this civilisation to develop its real tendencies, which were previously stifled, and which must run in the direction of social progress. In other words, Western civilisation is to be accepted as it is, for, once separated from the political interests that have led it astray, it can serve even better the interests of socialist society.

In this matter — and we shall see later on what the consequences were — Lenin remains essentially subject to a certain "Eurocentrism" in Marxist doctrine.[9] For Lenin, Russia is a "semi-civilised" country because it is "semi-Asiatic", half sunk in "barbarism", and it is this distinctiveness that, basically, constitutes its problems.

> "Look at the map of the R.S.F.S.R. There is room for dozens of large civilised states in those vast areas which lie to the north of Vologda, the south-east of Rostov-on-Don and Saratov, the south of Orenburg and Omsk, and the north of Tomsk. They are a realm of patriarchalism and semi- and downright barbarism. And what about the peasant backwoods of the rest of Russia, where scores of versts of country track, or rather of trackless country, lie between the villages and the railways, i.e., the material link with the big cities, large-scale industry, capitalism and culture? Isn't that also an area of wholesale patriarchalism,[10] and semi-barbarism?"[11]

This Russia must raise itself into industrial and technological civilisation, the condition *sine qua non* for the realisation of socialism. The problem and the aim are clear, but the attainment of the aim is hard; it means a long period filled with the "vast amount of urgent spade-work" that Russia still has to do "to reach the standard of an ordinary West-European civilised country".[12]

It is at this level that Lenin sees the cultural revolution as occurring, its tasks being "to create the fundamental requisites of civilisation".[13] The extraordinary thing about the Russian Revolution is just this inversion, in the actual course of history, of the historical process which Marx and Engels theorised about. The political and social revolution did not break out first in the "civilised" countries but in the most barbarous country, in Europe's "prison house of peoples". It is this phenomenon, this "remarkable combination of circumstances", as he calls it, that makes Lenin say that, since the political and social revolution has, in Russia, preceded the cultural revolution, all that is needed for the country to be regarded as fully socialist is for the cultural revolution to be carried through.

Thus, socialism is, for Russia, to be synonymous with accession to the ranks of the civilised countries, which are recognised above all by their highly-developed productive forces, the superiority of their science and technology and the high degree of rationality in their organisation of labour, with a set of patterns of behaviour which are expressions of this. It is clear that at the back of Lenin's mind is the idea that the cultural revolution, at this level, is a conjunctural requirement which has no necessary part in the revolutionary process. In other words, since culture, defined in this way, is, after all, the highest product of the development of industrial capitalism, no cultural revolution (with this still understood as signifying a revolution *of* and *in* civilisation) would have been called for if the proletarian revolution had occurred first, as it "should have", in such countries as Britain or Germany.

In those countries, civilisation is *already present* and does not need to be invented or re-invented: it is to be taken as it is.

> "The only socialism we can imagine is one based on all the lessons learned through large-scale capitalist culture. Socialism without postal and telegraph services, without machines, is the emptiest of phrases."[14]

What is required is for the exploited masses to become the immediate beneficiaries of this civilisation by making themselves masters of it. For Lenin, however, this accession to culture as civilisation does not take place at that level, but at the level of knowledge. As we shall see later on, it comes, for him, as the *direct* result of acquisition of culture-as-knowledge. *This* is the line that leads straight on to culture-as-civilisation.

However, while history's caprice obliges the youthful revolution to lay the foundations of civilisation in Russia, it enables the revolution, at the same time, to make a sort of historical short-cut, for it is a "workers' and peasants'" government that is to carry through this "titanic task". Thus, this "semi-civilisation", or "semi-barbarism", of the country of the revolution is found at once to be superior by virtue of its *political form*, the function of which is to express the will and aspirations of a people to win freedom for itself. And this political form is also the translation into practice of an ideology that has been put into effect for the very first time.

2. CULTURE AS IDEOLOGY

A passage that Lenin wrote well before the October

revolution shows clearly how he relates culture to ideology: "The *elements* of democratic and socialist culture are present, if only in rudimentary form, in *every* national culture, since in *every* nation there are toiling and exploited masses, whose conditions of life inevitably give rise to the ideology of democracy and socialism. But *every* nation also possesses a bourgeois culture (and most nations a reactionary and clerical culture as well) in the form, not merely of 'elements', but of the *dominant* culture".[15]

This sense of the word "culture" is, in Lenin's view, the only one that justifies making a distinction between bourgeois culture and proletarian culture, since these are based on different conceptions and pictures of the world, reflecting in each case consciousness determined by the place and function — ruling or ruled, exploiting or exploited — that the particular class holds in the world.[16]

It is no longer a question of a "pattern" to be followed, but, on the contrary, of something that is to be rejected and fought against. The clash between the two ideologies is, in the strict sense of the expression, a fight to the death, and one that often proves difficult, since the bourgeois culture-as-ideology survives for an indefinite period the overthrow of its conditions of existence, thanks to the widely-diffused strength of its implantation — in most cases unconscious — in the minds of those very men and women who wish to free themselves from its thraldom. At this level, too, the cultural revolution is an inescapable necessity, and can be described as a duel with that "other" who is also oneself.

Nevertheless, we never find appearing in Lenin the central idea of the Chinese cultural revolution, (what is undoubtedly its most original contribution) namely, the need for a specific struggle to be waged on the actual terrain of culture-as-ideology. For Lenin, the victory, and the strengthening, of the proletarian culture-as-ideology, is to result not so much from its own resistance to the assaults, open or insidious, of the bourgeois culture-as-ideology, as from the capacity of the proletarian government, and, in particular, of the Communist Party, to develop the material foundation and productivity of the new regime — large-scale industry, and the organisation of labour which follows from this. Lenin did not hesitate, for example, to say that it was necessary to talk politics less, to have fewer excited debates and theoretical speeches, and to concern oneself more with tasks, even very petty ones, in the economic sphere.[17]

In order to accomplish these tasks, what the Soviet masses lacked, above all, as Lenin saw it, was not culture-as-ideology but rather culture-as-knowledge. Basically, so far as Lenin was concerned, the problem of culture-as-ideology had been solved, in the main, the moment the masses took power — as soon, in fact, as, despite the petty-bourgeois waverings that would still remain possible for a long time yet, the ideological continuity of the political line was in the safe hands of the Communist Party.[18] In a passage of 1918 Lenin gives an explanation of the occurrence of the Russian Revolution and of its special difficulties which seems to me essential for understanding his thought on this question:

"The whole difficulty of the Russian revolution is that *it was much easier for the Russian revolutionary working class to start* than it is for the West European classes, but *it is much more difficult for us to continue*. It is more difficult to start a revolution in West-European countries because there the revolutionary proletariat is opposed by the higher thinking that comes with culture, while the working class is in a state of cultural slavery."[19]

In this passage we see again the distinction, already noted, which Lenin makes between culture (civilisation and knowledge) and the (ideological) use that is made of it. The latter, "cultural slavery", is all the more effective and, therefore, all the harder to uproot because it results from a higher development of capitalism and so, for Lenin, of civilisation and culture. This is why it is "more difficult" for the Western working class to "start a revolution", but, for the *very same reason*, it will be much easier for them to continue it, because, for them, civilisation and culture are *already present*, and *all that is needed* is to appropriate these and put them "at the service of the masses". For the inverse reason, the great "strength" of the Russian proletariat *before* the taking of power implies the very great difficulties, and accounts for the extreme fragility of its rule, experienced *after* that event. If the Russian proletariat was, in a certain way, "ideologically" stronger, that was because it was "culturally" (in senses 1 and 3) to an infinite degree weaker. Therefore Lenin never tires of repeating that the crucial problem lies in acquiring culture-as-knowledge. If the Russian revolution wants to survive, then it must mobilise all its forces to acquire this culture. In comparison with this vital task, everything else, and especially "pretensions" to trying to create a proletarian culture, looks to Lenin like so much rhetoric that is beyond the revolution's means, waste of time and energy, even a diversion that harms the interests of the revolution. First and foremost, it is necessary to "teach the Russian savage",[20] and, to that end, to begin at the beginning, by teaching him to read and write.

3. CULTURE AS KNOWLEDGE

This third meaning, which is the one found most often in Lenin's writings, recurs indefatigably, and, in his last writings especially, becomes a veritable obsession: it is necessary to learn, learn and keep on learning. The point being that, he says, "it takes knowledge to participate in the revolution with intelligence, purpose and success".[21]

It is primarily important to acquire that first degree of culture, elementary instruction, the lack of which weighs like a fatality upon the birth of the revolution; but, at the same time, under the new conditions, a formidable thirst for knowledge awakens, proportionate to this "barbaric" illiteracy. Therefore, without reducing culture to instruction, Lenin stresses what, for him, is the fundamental meaning of the concept of culture, namely, knowledge, the aggregate of what mankind knows, that "general culture" which is the appanage of "civilised" societies. And Lenin singles out, to assign them a special, preponderant position, science and technology, so that he is led sometimes to identify culture-as-knowledge purely and simply with scientific and technological knowledge. This is, indeed, one of his main preoccupations. Science and technology, that is what we lack, that is what we need. The data of the problem are obvious; no revolution without developed industry, no developed industry without modern science and technology. To Lenin's famous formula: "electrification plus Soviet power equals socialism" corresponds this other formula which merely explains it: in order to ensure the irreversible success of Soviet construction, "industry ... must be rehabilitated on the basis of modern technology, which means the electrification of industry and a higher culture".[22]

Now, knowledge, scientific and technological knowledge, is an achievement of advanced capitalism: long the privileged possession of a minority, all that is needed now is for it to be taken over, for the masses to be enabled to get at it. Lenin's view on this point is categorical: there are not two possible paths. To talk in this connexion of a proletarian culture, to be invented in opposition to bourgeois culture, is theoretical nonsense, irresponsible revolutionary "childishness". There is no culture but bourgeois culture, an acquisition by mankind which must not, cannot be rejected if one wants to build communism. At this level there is no mention of any need for a cultural revolution: the stress is laid, in Lenin's writings, firmly upon the assimilation of bourgeois culture, even upon "apprenticeship" to it, rather than upon transformation of this culture. In other words, strictly speaking that is just what the cultural revolution means: the accession of the masses to culture-as-knowledge, or, what is the same thing, the "democratisation" of this culture, which, as we have seen already, is, in Lenin's eyes, the stage that has to be traversed in order to attain civilisation. It seems, indeed, that, for Lenin, if there is such a thing as a cultural revolution, then it consists in this "transformation by quantity" which takes place automatically as soon as the masses gain access to bourgeois culture, master it, and "transform" it from the instrument for ruling them which it was into an instrument for freeing them.

"In the old days, human genius, the brain of man, created only to give some the benefits of technology and culture, and to deprive others of the bare necessities, education and development. From now on, all the marvels of science and the gains of culture belong to the nation as a whole, and never again will man's brain and human genius be used for oppression and exploitation."[23]

What counts, in the given situation, is to know to whom this "bourgeois" culture henceforth belongs: to know, in other words, who holds power. So long as the Soviets rule, the adjective "bourgeois" in the expression "bourgeois culture" will be entirely relative in meaning.

"For a start", writes Lenin, "we should be satisfied with real bourgeois culture; for a start, we should be glad to dispense with the cruder types of pre-bourgeois culture, i.e., bureaucratic or serf culture, etc."[24]

When "that" culture has been acquired and assimilated, it will be more "Soviet" than "bourgeois", and the victory of the revolution will be guaranteed.

What needs now to be determined is the nature of this assimilation process, for the question remains to be answered — what is it that must be assimilated (everything? or only a part?) and, above all, *how* is it to be assimilated? Lenin is fully aware that he is faced here with a quite original problem, which has to be solved at once if the revolution is not to suffer defeat, but for the solution of which one cannot refer to a single socialist work "or the opinion of a single prominent socialist on future society which pointed to this concrete, practical difficulty that would confront the working class when it took power, when it set itself the task of turning the sum total of the very rich, historically inevitable and necessary for us store of culture and knowledge and technique accumulated by capitalism from an instrument of capitalism into an instrument of socialism".[25]

It is interesting to observe that Lenin had begun to answer these questions as far back as 1897, in a work with the significant title: *The Heritage We Renounce.*

C. *Problems of inheritance*

1. THE HERITAGE

Lenin takes up, where this matter is concerned, a particularly clear-cut position, on which he was never to feel the need to go back: it seems to him so absolutely correct because it is the only practical one: "We must take the entire culture that capitalism left behind and build socialism with it. We must take all its science, technology, knowledge and art. Without these we shall be unable to build communist society."[26]

For Lenin, accordingly, the problem is not one of deciding what line to follow on this question: that, for him, is self-evident, to the exclusion of any other line. The only problem, for him, is how to convince of this the masses in general, and the Communists in particular.

"If you are unable to errect the edifice with the materials bequeathed to us by the bourgeois world, you will not be able to build it at all, and you will not be Communists, but mere phrasemongers. For the purpose of building socialism we must make the fullest use of the science, technology and, in general, everything that capitalist Russia bequeathed to us."[27]

In order to justify and illustrate his view, Lenin appeals to the example of Marx himself, who "shows how communism arose out of the sum of human knowledge". This enables him, at the same time, to present his idea more subtly: Marx, he says "critically reshaped everything that had been created by human society, without ignoring a single detail".[28] The assimilation must therefore be critical: it must retain that which is "most valuable" in capitalism, the entire product of what Lenin calls "progressive capitalism". In other words, the problem of the heritage is, in the last analysis, the problem of a critical approach to it, and, still more profoundly, of the nature of this critical approach. The fact that Lenin shows himself so circumspect on this point is already, in itself, a pointer to the problem. Furthermore, the use of the expression "proletarian culture" at the three levels mentioned, but especially in the third sense, is mainly a matter, with him, of the polemical procedure which consists in adopting, so as the better to refute them, the very concepts used by his opponents. Thus, in order to understand what Lenin means by "criticism" we need to refer to what he puts forward as the only possible definition of "proletarian culture", namely: "Proletarian culture must be the logical development of the store of knowledge mankind has accumulated under the yoke of capitalist, landowner and bureaucratic society".[29]

It is noteworthy that Lenin does not describe this development as dialectical or contradictory, but as "logical", which indicates continuity rather than a break or a change, and shows the narrow limits confining the *critical* element in the assimilation he advocates. A literal translation of the Russian expression rendered here as "logical development" brings this out even more clearly. *Zakonomernoye razvitiye* means, precisely: development which is normal, in conformity with objective laws, regular, legitimate. We now see better that, for Lenin, the process by which the cultural heritage takes, to some extent, a new course, on the basis of its assimilation by the masses, obeys certain "objective", historically necessary laws, which by their very existence reduce considerably any possibility of a voluntary intervention "from without", aimed at giving direction to this process. It is therefore not surprising that the demand for criticism grows dim, most of the time, in comparison with the repeated assertion of the need for complete assimilation.

This conception of an objective process is merely the general expression of the idea which emerges more or less clearly from all of Lenin's writings, that *not all culture* is burdened with ideology. There is, it might be said, a gradual "cleansing" from ideology as one moves from one sphere to another in culture — from what it is conventional to call the human sciences (especially philosophy, history and economics), which are deeply impregnated with ideology, through artistic creation, in which the "coefficient" of ideology is extremely variable, to the realm of science and technology, which would appear to be somehow entirely free from ideology. On scientific and technological culture Lenin's ideas are especially striking, above all when one knows the role which he assigned to this: "We shall be able to build up Communism only when, with the means provided by bourgeois science and technology, we make it more accessible to the people. There is no other way of building a Communist society".[30]

It seems, indeed, that for him *this* culture can be charged with being "bourgeois" only in so far as the interests it serves — or, in the case of Russia, *has* served — are those of the bourgeoisie. In other words, it is not this culture that is ideological, but the use made of it.[31] Taking this reasoning further, one might say that scientific and technological culture is purely a tool — the terminology used by Lenin is revealing in this respect: "bricks", "materials", etc. — a sort of neutral entity the function of which can change depending on the use being made of it, without its necessarily changing its nature. At this level there is no need for any "cleansing" or any "critical reshaping". *This* heritage is to be taken over completely, and as soon as possible. Scientific and technological culture *as such* is vital to the revolutionary process, just as it was to the development and consolidation of the bourgeoisie. And from being "bourgeois", as it was under the regime now abolished, it becomes, with the accession to power of the Soviets, *automatically* revolutionary (note that Lenin never says "proletarian"). So that when Lenin applies the epithet "bourgeois" to the terms "science" and "technology" this is done, it seems to me, with a dual significance — to refer to the science and technology developed by the bourgeoisie (the only kind existing) and to refer to the science and technology which the new society does not yet possess.

The urgent question is therefore to take over *this* culture as quickly as can be — but also, more generally, to take over *all* culture in the third sense, since, on the one hand, it determines both of the other levels, and since, on the other hand, without it, Lenin insists, the masses will always remain incapable of really managing their own affairs: "The result of this low cultural level is that the Soviets, which by virtue of their programme are organs of government *by the working people*, are in fact organs of government *for the working people* by the advanced section of the proletariat, but not by the working people as a whole".[32]

And just because it has been for centuries the privilege of a minority and the "speciality" of certain men, this culture is to be taken from where it is to be found, namely in the heads of the specialists, that is, in general, among the "bourgeois" intellectuals, whom the workers, says Lenin, need henceforth to "guard as the apple of their eye".[33]

2. THE "BEARERS" OF CULTURE

The line to be pursued in relation to the bourgeois intellectuals, the representatives and wielders *par excellence* of "culture", follows easily from all that has just been said, and links up logically with the problematic of

the heritage. Lenin defends this line with a fury that is all
the more stubborn because, in his eyes, these "specialists"
are the most finished concrete manifestation of the
capitalist heritage, and so the only persons who can make
effective and immediate the utilisation of this heritage.
And the Russian Revolution is faced with an imperative
necessity that is as simple to state as it is difficult to
accomplish, namely, to act practically without losing any
time.

> "Capitalism has left us a valuable legacy in the shape
> of its biggest experts. And we must be sure to utilise
> them, and utilise them on a broad and mass scale;
> we must put every one of them to work. We have no
> time to spend on training experts from among our
> own Communists, because everything depends on
> practical work and practical results."[34]

It remains the fact, nevertheless, that the intellectuals are
marked with contradiction due to their place in the
system from which they have emerged. On the one hand,
they have been formed precisely by and in this system, the
ideological values of which they inevitably carry with
them. They are indeed the heirs of the old society and,
according to Lenin, they are characterised above all by
their "lack of firmness". The fact is, he says, "educated
people yield to the policy and influence of the bourgeoisie
because they acquired all their education in a bourgeois
environment and from that environment. That is why
they stumble at every step and make political concessions
to the counter-revolutionary bourgeoisie".[35]
   But this means, at the same time, that one cannot
confuse culture (in the third sense) with the "bourgeois

environment", or the ruling ideology. The one is, to be sure, dependent on the other (though we have seen within what narrow limits Lenin thinks this applies in the case of science and technology), but they are *not* reducible one to the other.

On the other hand, the intellectuals are, for Lenin, no less victims of bourgeois ideology than they are its bearers. Only a section of them are lost to the revolution. And since they are victims, themselves exploited by the regime, the emancipation of the proletariat is, or ought to be, that of the intellectuals as well, for "these experts are not the servitors of the exploiters, they are active cultural workers, who in bourgeois society served the bourgeoisie, and of whom all socialists all over the world said that in a proletarian society they would serve *us*".[36]

This contradiction gives rise to a dual attitude. Since the revolution cannot be safeguarded by "some new men or other", says Lenin, we must make all the specialists, that is, all the intellectuals, work for the good of the revolution, and learn from them while surrounding them with a "proletarian environment", in an atmosphere of fraternal collaboration, providing them with the best possible material conditions. On this last point Lenin is perfectly aware of "the corrupting influence of high salaries ... upon the Soviet authorities",[37] and the abandonment of a principle which this represents. The only way to counteract the harmful effects is, he says, not to conceal this fact from the masses, to prove by so doing the confidence that we have in them, and to appeal to their consciousness and discipline. We have to learn along with them and to explain to them, without trying to disguise reality, that this is a very heavy tribute which has to be paid, but one which cannot be avoided if they are to acquire knowledge and bring the specialists into their service.

The aim, in the long run, is to induce the intellectuals gradually to alter their attitude towards the proletarian power: this is to be done by accepting them as they are, without requiring from them any allegiance on a basis of principle and remaining satisfied with a co-operative neutrality on their part.

"These people are accustomed to do cultural work, they advanced it within the framework of the bourgeois system, that is, they enriched the bourgeoisie with tremendous material acquisitions, but gave them to the proletariat in infinitesimal doses — nevertheless they did advance culture, that was their job. As they see the working class promoting organised and advanced sections, which not only value culture but also help to convey it to the people, they are changing their attitude towards us".[38]

All measures of a coercive nature are to be ruled out: they may even prove counter-productive, and will certainly always do so in the long run. It is necessary to win the intellectuals over by example, to win them *morally*: the regime of the big stick, as Lenin himself puts it, has never produced any but poisoned fruits. The masses, and the workers in particular, must understand that, in this matter, violence and constraint work against the proletarian power, that they testify not to its strength but to its weakness. If it wishes to ensure the stability of its dictatorship, the proletariat must not turn against itself the powerful weapon of culture. In order to wield this weapon, the only means available is to assimilate the knowledge possessed by the bourgeois specialists.[39] In short, Lenin declares, we must learn from them, become apprentices to them, showing patience and modesty. "Our Party is waging and will continue to wage 'a relentless struggle against the pseudo-radical but actually ignorant and conceited opinion that the working people are capable of overcoming capitalism and the bourgeois social system without learning from bourgeois specialists, without making use of their services and without undergoing the *training of a lengthy period* of work side by side with them'."[40]

This apprenticeship is not, to be sure, conceived as a one-way affair: it is necessary to learn from the bourgeois specialists while at the same time helping *them* to learn from the proletariat. Each of these two sides of the affair is equally important, however. The metaphor of construction, of building work, is constantly repeated: the specialists provide the bricks, the proletariat provides the builders. "We have bourgeois experts and nothing else. We have no other bricks with which to build."[41] It is for the masses to lay the bricks, in accordance with a definite plan and although, in the end, what the building will be like depends on them, the idea that inspires them will remain a mere pious aspiration unless they provide themselves with the means to realise it, namely, bourgeois culture in the third sense, together with the intellectuals inherited from capitalism. "The idea that we can build Communism with the aid of pure Communists, without the assistance of bourgeois experts, is childish ... We must set them to work *as a technical and cultural force* so as to preserve them and to transform an uncultured and barbarian capitalist country into a cultured, communist country".[42] "Every expert must be treasured as being the only vehicle of technology and culture, without whom there can be nothing, without whom there can be no communism."[43]

In Lenin's mind this problem is of first-class

importance. Every day won for the revolution confirms him in his conviction that all the goodwill of the proletariat, all its courage and self-sacrifice, all its creative abilities are proving inadequate for the building of the new society, that its forces are incapable, on their own, of bringing the revolution to final victory: that, in the last analysis, the essence of the proletariat's role is not so much to be the sole effective *executant* of the revolution as to show that it is the only true *guide* thereof. And it is the vanguard of the proletariat which, by virtue of its very position, must, more than any other section, grasp this idea.

"We shall never rely on the intellectuals, we shall only rely on the vanguard of the proletariat that leads all workers and poor peasants. The Communist Party can rely on no other support. It is one thing, however, to rely on the class which embodies the dictatorship, and another to dominate over other classes ... The class-conscious proletariat's job now is to appreciate that its domination does not mean carrying out all the tasks itself."[44]

3. FIRST CRITICAL COMMENTS

This conception of the "heritage" presents, however, more problems than it solves. It leaves out of the problematic the question of the critical element, with which Lenin hardly troubles himself, essentially offering only formal phrases such as his condemnation of mere book-learning, of stuffing one's head with rubbish, and so on. "'assimilating critically" means, above all, for Lenin, "not cramming your mind with useless lumber".[45] And this framework, already narrow, within which the critical attitude is to be confined, turns out to be still further restricted by another determination, which tells all the more gravely because it usually remains hidden — even from Lenin himself, to some extent. This second determination (or, more precisely, predetermination) shows itself when we analyse Lenin's many references to Marx. These might, at first glance, be taken as constituting an exhortation to act "like Marx", to take nothing as it stands but to subject everything to *one's own* criticism. However, this possible first interpretation fades away as we look more closely, giving place to another one, which emerges finally as the key to Lenin's thought on this matter: the essential work of criticism has already been done by Marx, who has re-thought *everything*, "without ignoring a single detail". This idea is revealed unequivocally in Lenin's note *On Proletarian Culture*, in which he declares that "the Marxist world-outlook is *the only true expression* of the interests, the viewpoint, and the culture of the revolutionary proletariat" and that "*only further work on this basis and in this direction* ... can be recognised as the development of a genuine proletarian culture".[46] This idea is also given synthetic expression in another of Lenin's formulations, as lapidary in form as it was pregnant with possible consequences: "*Not special ideas, but Marxism*".[47] Independently of Lenin's will, there is here, in germ, it seems to me, a dogmatising of Marxism, which is elevated into a universal and all-sufficient "answer" — the opening of the gate to sacralisation of the allegedly Marxist point of view (that which is, in all circumstances, "on the line", and for which the use made of the ritual formulas measures the value of what is said), and to its corollary in practice, the mystique of monolithic unity, which is valued for its own sake more than for the principles it is supposed to unify. I say "in germ" because, both in practical activity and in theoretical thinking, and among the leaders as well as among the advanced elements of the masses, the lines of force of the reality of the 1920s — this can never be recalled too often — ran, fundamentally, in the direction of a re-considering of most of these problems, a search for new and untried paths. That was a world in a state of creative ferment, in constant motion, to which Lenin's thought contributed its share of leaven along with many others. It nevertheless remains true that, as regards the problematic under review; Lenin fell into the error, which he himself condemned[48] of treating Marx's doctrine as "something completed and inviolable", or, at least, as the necessary and sufficient foundation from which it was futile to depart in one's questioning of reality. [49] Here, too, the underlying idea, determining all the rest, is that it is enough to use what is "already present", and that to "waste" time in seeking elsewhere and for something different is a useless luxury for the revolution. And so we come back to the general observations made at the beginning of this first part of the book, and touch on one of the essential components of Lenin's conceptions of culture and of the "heritage", which are closely interconnected. The angle from which Lenin looks at the problem is that of the man of action, the revolutionary leader (*leader of the Party and of the State*), faced with a situation that calls for *practical and immediate solutions*. Hence, inevitably, the essential characteristic of his conception, its pragmatic nature, particularly obvious in relation to culture-as-knowledge, which for the same reasons Lenin sees as the touchstone of the general problem of culture in connexion with the revolution. The idea (a very topical one, incidentally) that underlies this outlook is that knowledge, especially science and technology, is a form of power which is among the most effective created by class society.

Therefore, so long as the proletariat has not equipped itself with this power, so long as it has not become *cultured*, the "vicious circle" of the Russian Revolution cannot be broken. On the one hand, the political power that has just been established provides the proletariat at once with the conditions for acceding to that particular form of power called knowledge, in relation to which the proletariat has hitherto lived in a veritable ghetto. On the other hand, political and economic power will not become really and effectively proletarian until the proletariat has mastered knowledge, until the day comes when it can do without the "bourgeois specialists". I shall return in the second part of the book to these questions of prime importance. It can, however, be suggested here and now that Lenin's obsession with consolidating the revolution as quickly as possible at its weakest link,[50] cultural backwardness, by seizing, just as one seizes power, the "only culture that exists", bourgeois culture, causes him to overlook, so to speak, a vital fact. Marx and Engels stressed this fact, in *The German Ideology* for instance, namely, that even the "purest" of sciences (they were, in the course of their criticism of Feuerbach, referring to natural science) "is provided with an aim, as with its material, only through trade and industry, through the sensuous activity of men",[51] and that, consequently, all culture is ideological in so far as it represents no less the sum of the *questions* that a society asks itself at a certain stage of its history than it does the sum of the *answers* given. It is not a matter of enclosing in an ignorant determinism the complex dialectical interplay, referred to in the introduction, which governs the relationship between culture and the material activity from which it arises, with which it is organically linked, but upon which — a dialectical "moment" that is too often forgotten — it in turn reacts. I want merely to point out that this complexity means, precisely, that these links are especially well hidden, that they are the least obvious to "the naked eye", and exist at such varied levels of connexion that, if one can put it like this, they enable a Lenin and a Feuerbach to agree in affirming that science and technology, (if not all knowledge in general), in the one case, and natural science, in the other, are "pure". This *rapprochement* of Lenin and Feuerbach suffers, no doubt, from all the simplifications it presumes, but all that is meant by it is this: relentlessly importuned by an urgent need for "culture", Lenin came, as it were, to make a virtue of necessity, relegating to the realm of Utopia the desire to apply to the sphere of culture what he himself, following Marx, had said was the basic lesson of the Paris Commune during its ill-starred experience of power, namely, that "the working class cannot simply lay hold of the ready-made state machinery and wield it for its own purposes".[52]

Lenin's conceptions possess the inestimable merit of not encouraging the sterile manicheism and the policy of anathema which were to enjoy so prosperous a future in Soviet official pronouncements from the 1930s onward, and from which the Cultural Revolution in China seems not to have been free, either. But this does not, in my view, prevent them from avoiding the basic question, namely, the nature of the process involved in the assimilation of "bourgeois culture". The problem must not and cannot be presented in terms of a dichotomy: either take everything or reject everything. In short, Lenin's analysis is faulty, at bottom, through want of dialectics.

Finally, in order to arrive at an overall under-standing of Lenin's ideas concerning this problematic, we need to set them again in their own polemical context. It is this context that explains, in particular, the tone of many of Lenin's writings, a tone which in itself is symptomatic of the importance he gave to what was at stake in the debate. He engages in this discussion as in a battle which must be fought, and which absolutely must be won, and a knowledge of the ideas he is combating so stubbornly gives us another approach to a knowledge of the ideas he is defending.

III. LENIN AGAINST PROLETARIAN CULTURE

We have already seen that Lenin rejects the very concept of "proletarian culture", although he does make use of the expression, mainly for a polemical purpose. Lenin's theses were advanced in opposition to adversaries, mentioned by name, whose cohesion was based not only on theoretical agreement among themselves but also on a structured organisation, *Proletkult*,[53] which took upon itself the task of imposing and putting into practice the ideas they upheld. It is especially difficult to follow as one ought this great theoretical debate, which nevertheless occupies, directly or indirectly, an important place in the last phase of Lenin's work, to which it often provides the back-cloth. Under cover of Lenin's thought, this debate has been relegated, like so many others, by Soviet historiography since the 1930s, to the *oubliettes* of official thought, put into the inaccessible dossiers of those matters, finally filed away, on which the textbooks of philosophy and history are considered to tell the reader all he needs to know. The principal theoretician of the *Proletkult* movement, Bogdanov, was, of course, the first victim of this policy, which turned him into an "idealist" and "subjectivist" who was "objectively" counter-revolutionary. I can only express regret here for the inevitable gaps in this exposition due to the fact that Bogdanov's writings, and in particular those on culture and the cultural revolution, have in the main been translated only into German, in so far as they are not totally unknown. Long before the organised existence of *Proletkult*, which appeared in September 1917, Bogdanov had begun, very early, to maintain the need for a simultaneous cultural revolution, linked with the economic and political revolutions, but developing specific features and enjoying a certain autonomy in relation to them. The originality of *Proletkult* from the standpoint of theory lay not so much in its assertion of this relative autonomy of the cultural sphere as in its determination of the specific character of this sphere as one of the special areas of the class struggle which continues, even more intense than before, after the political overthrow of the bourgeoisie.[54] This characterisation of the cultural sphere dictates, according to the *Proletkult* theory, a differentiated, specific form of activity in this sphere, which is seen as the last bastion and last refuge of the bourgeoisie in retreat.[55] The other notable feature of *Proletkult*, from the practical standpoint, lies in its organisation, which included social, political and cultural elements, and to which a very large number of Bolsheviks adhered. The fact that many members of the Bolshevik Party supported the theses of *Proletkult*, and even joined the organisation, testifies to the echo that *Proletkult's* ideas found even among a group of persons already moulded politically, and accounts for the vehemence, even brutality, of Lenin's attacks on the movement.

The fundamental objective of *Proletkult* was "to create a new class culture, 'proletarian culture' ". Starting from the Marxist premise that social existence determines consciousness, *Proletkult* sets forth the following schema of the process that historical development should follow:

Thesis = bourgeois culture
Antithesis = proletarian class culture
Synthesis (under socialism) = universal human culture.

On the *second* stage after the capture of power, the synthesis, a culture that would be truly human, since it would be the reflexion of a classless society, agreement was unanimous, as has been said: the problem was to decide what would, or should, be the "moment" of antithesis. The members of *Proletkult* defended themselves against the charge of advocating the policy of the "clean sweep", seeking to destroy all the values of the past because these were inevitably bourgeois.

> "Our task is not to destroy the material values of the old culture, but to destroy the ideology, the foundation, on which these values have developed."[56]

It is thus plain that the problematic set forth by *Proletkult* differs completely from Lenin's analysis, in that it merges into one the three levels I have distinguished (ideology, civilisation, knowledge) and reduces the problem of culture to its ideological substructure.[57] Whereas, for Lenin, this question solves itself, so to speak, once the political form within which it is presented is proletarian, and once the masses gain access to "bourgeois" knowledge, for *Proletkult*, on the contrary, the line of development runs in almost the opposite direction. According to them, it is incompatible with the proletarian nature of the government that the masses (and even less the proletariat itself) should wish to dominate culture, becoming its masters and creators, without necessarily proceeding first of all (or, more precisely, at the same time), to re-examine, from the angle of the new class ideology, the (bourgeois-ideological) values which underlie all previously-existing culture. In other words, according to *Proletkult*, the same culture cannot serve different interests: bourgeois culture cannot serve the interests of the proletarian regime without calling in question the advances made by this regime, and its very nature.[58] Thus, there is no single cultural domain that can escape from this inexorable "law" — neither art nor science and technology, and the latter less, perhaps, than any other. *Proletkult*, like Lenin, accords a preponderant role to science in the building of socialism, but this agreement in principle leads them once again to divergent conclusions. We have seen that, for Lenin, science is, as it were, ideologically neutral, since its distinctive requirements by their very nature place it on a level of objectivity such that it can escape from class determinations. *Proletkult's* attitude is the reverse of this: because science (and consequently technology, which is indissociable from it) is bound up with material production, it cannot be taken as it stands, but must be subjected to a modification, or rather a "revolutionisation", from within. It must, in short, become "proletarian".

"The programmes of the socialist parties set themselves the task of democratising science, but what we see as necessary is its socialisation, its collectivisation. What does this mean? Democratisation enlarges for the masses the area of mastery of bourgeois science, both in breadth and in depth, but this science as such remains unaffected. The collectivisation of science affects also its essence, method, form and scope. Our task consists in bringing the content and methods of science into line with the requirements of socialist production."[59]

On the one hand, this collectivisation of science will have as its first consequence the ending of the fragmentation of scientific knowledge, which results from the system of capitalist competition: it will help science to progress towards its "monism". On the other, it will create a new type of man, socialist man, who "cannot but be encyclopaedic, in the best sense of the word". To sum up, writes Pletnev, "without science socialism is impossible, and it is also impossible with *bourgeois* science".[60]

It is not hard to perceive that these so divergent theoretical positions imply totally opposed ideas as to the role that the proletariat can and must play in this process. Lenin, as we have seen, considers that the conscious proletariat shows proof of its maturity precisely when it acknowledges that it is incapable of building the new society relying on its own powers alone, without having recourse to bourgeois culture and bourgeois specialists — when it admits that it cannot be self-sufficient and lay claim to a proletarian purity that excludes any contribution from outside its ranks. For *Proletkult*, on the contrary, the new culture can be realised only by the forces of the proletariat itself. Like the bourgeoisie, the proletariat must form its own men of learning, its own specialists, for the entire spectrum of the cultural domain. It must count on itself alone: if the situation in Russia is such that the proletariat cannot yet do without all the specialists inherited from capitalism,[61] there can nevertheless be no question of trying to integrate them in proletarian society, and still less of learning from them. The proletarians, claimed *Proletkult*, are bearers of values specific to themselves, with which they must impregnate society as a whole. "The feeling of class solidarity, the 'we' feeling ... It is by this being that the class-consciousness of the proletariat is determined. It is alien to the peasant, to the bourgeois, to the intellectual — to the doctor, the lawyer, the engineer, educated in the principles of capitalist competition, of which the basis is 'I'."[62] Any intervention by any specialist whatsoever must, therefore, never be other than an exception to the rule. The bourgeois specialist is psychologically, organically incapable of serving the interests of the proletariat: at most, decrees *Proletkult*, he can accept Soviet power — he will never adhere to its Communist ideology.[63]

This outline of the principal theses of *Proletkult* enables us to measure the gap between them and Lenin. The ideas they embodied were not confined to *Proletkult*, and the discussion they aroused proves that they were closely bound up with the concerns and questions of the moment. They found defenders even in the leadership of the Bolshevik Party, and Bukharin (a former disciple of Bogdanov's), though he did not agree with all of the analyses made by *Proletkult*, constantly urged the creation of a culture that would be specific to the proletarian state:

"I think that we can and must try to bring it about, in every sphere of ideological and scientific power, even in mathematics, that we eventually have a certain approach which is specific to us. From this a new spirit will develop in cultural relations." [64]

Lenin's theoretical opposition nevertheless does not

satisfactorily account for his special hostility to
Proletkult. The whole period extending from the seizure
of power in October 1917 to the mid-1920s was marked
by an abundance of tendencies of the most varied kinds in
all spheres of cultural activity, an almost anarchic
ferment of ideas and a freedom of expression in cultural
creativity that was without precedent in history and has
remained without parallel ever since. But *Proletkult* was
the only movement among these many against which
Lenin called, several times, even going so far as to
intervene personally in the matter, for vigorous *administrative* measures. The point was that *Proletkult's* thesis on
the need for an autonomous and specific cultural
revolution led it to see itself as the only authentic driving
force, the only true guide, of the cultural movement. It
wanted, in short, to be in the cultural sphere what the
Bolshevik Party was in that of politics, making itself, at
that level, the instrument of the "dictatorship of the
proletariat" with a role corresponding to that which,
according to *Proletkult*, the Party played at the political
level.[65] This was why, however paradoxical it may seem
when we know what Lenin's attitude toward them was,
the followers of *Proletkult* constantly emphasised their
loyalty to the Bolshevik Party, and in particular to Lenin,
whom they saw as the most ardent defender of the
proletarian dictatorship. And here lies the key to Lenin's
anger. However opposed he might be to the theses of
Proletkult, Lenin could have confined himself to refuting
them on the theoretical level, without resort to measures
of coercion, or at least to denouncing these ideas in
unrestrained language, as stupid, fantastic, absurd, even
as a falsification of historical materialism. But he could
not, at any price, allow to develop, in a sphere so vital to
the revolution as that of culture, an organisation
claiming leadership in this sphere which was independent

of the Party and *outside control by the relevant State organ*, and which put forward ideas that, in Lenin's view, were so dangerous for the present and future of the revolution. *Proletkult* had become an immediate *political* threat, against which practical, administrative measures had to be taken without delay, since theoretical struggle was proving inadequate.

This recalling of the historical context, this succinct "history of ideas", has seemed necessary in order that we may arrive at an overall understanding of Lenin's ideas on culture and its relation to proletarian culture, in the elaboration and affirmation of which his struggle, theoretical and practical, against *Proletkult*, played an important part. Thus, the rough draft of a resolution on proletarian culture, which Lenin took time (something he never had too much of) to write out personally, in order to get it adopted at the First National Congress of *Proletkult*, offers us an exposition of Lenin's views which I think needs to be reproduced in full because it is a perfect synthesis of his fundamental ideas, at both the theoretical and the practical levels:

"1. Not special ideas, but Marxism.

2. Not the *invention* of a new proletarian culture, but the *development* of the best models, traditions and results of the *existing* culture, *from the point of view* of the Marxist world outlook and the conditions of life and struggle of the proletariat in the period of its dictatorship.

3. Not apart from the People's Commissariat for Education, but as part of it, since the R.C.P. [Russian Communist Party] + Commissariat for Education = Σ *Proletkult*.

4. *Proletkult's* close link with and subordination to the Commissariat for Education."[66]

I have already commented on what Lenin's propositions contain, in germ, of the dogmatisation of Marxism, and the way in which they actually deny the need to take up an original and critical attitude corresponding to the originality of any proletarian revolution in general, and of the Russian revolution in particular. In this sense, I think, *Proletkult* must be allowed the merit of having advocated the need for a creative appropriation of culture by the masses, indissociable from its radical transformation, that is, the transformation of the ideological basis of culture in class society. Unfortunately, while *Proletkult* raised this important problem, it did so *in a dogmatic way* that was expressed practically in a sectarianism which was not to be found at all in the policy advocated and applied by Lenin and the Bolshevik Party. Indeed, though Lenin shows a pronounced tendency to treat Marxism as *the* (necessary and sufficient) form of criticism, he never claims, as *Proletkult* tended to do, that culture can be reduced to Marxism, nor that it is enough to have mastered Marxism in order to become a revolutionary and a Communist, or to instruct the masses in it in order that they may attain the "enlightenment" of revolutionary truth. The following passages, taken from two of Lenin's writings, express in a straightforward way what he thought on that matter: "If the study of communism consisted solely in assimilating what is contained in communist books and pamphlets, we might all too easily obtain Communist text-jugglers or braggarts". "It would be the biggest and most grievous mistake a Marxist could make to think that the millions of the people (especially the peasants and artisans), who have been condemned by all modern society to darkness, ignorance and superstition, can extricate themselves from this darkness only along the straight line of a purely Marxist education."[67]

Furthermore, one of the weak points in the position of *Proletkult* (and at the same time one of the sources of its sectarianism), which Lenin did not fail constantly to remind his readers of, was its reduction of "the masses" to "the proletariat" — a reduction which Lenin said was all the more unforgivable in a country where the population included four times as many peasants as proletarians. Finally, Lenin considered (rightly, in my view), that *Proletkult* was making a serious mistake in denying that any positive role in the accomplishment of the revolution could be played by anyone who could not boast a proletarian origin or who, in general, did not "recognise" the Communist ideology. "One of the biggest and most dangerous mistakes made by Communists (as generally by revolutionaries who have successfully accomplished the beginning of a revolution) is the idea that a revolution can be made by revolutionaries alone ... Without an alliance with non-Communists in the most diverse spheres of activity there can be no question of any successful communist construction."[68]

In this first part of the book my task has been to set forth as fully as possible, in the form of textual analysis, Lenin's thought, which I have characterised as "the dominant point of view" of his period, for these two reasons: first, that this was the point of view that imposed itself during the 1920s and, second, because it was this that, *to a certain extent*, provided the basis and backing for the subsequent development of official thought which it is conventional to call "Stalinism". In the second part I shall seek to reveal and to analyse the assumptions which predetermined Lenin's thinking (and, consequently, the dominant thinking of his time), and to define the influence that they had upon the development referred to. I shall try, in short, to see in what way this point of view of Lenin's, the "dominant" point of view, was itself "dominated".

NOTES

1 Lenin, *Collected Works*, 4th edition, English version (henceforth referred to as *C.W.*) Vol.33, p.480.

2 N.I. Bukharin, *Lenin As A Marxist* (17 February 1924), London, C.P.G.B. 1925, p.54. (The published translation is somewhat crude. For "definite succession" read "a certain continuity": *Trans.*)

3 *C.W.*, Vol. 25, p.385: *The State and Revolution*, August-September 1917.

4 E.g.: *The Immediate Tasks of the Soviet Government*, March-April 1918: *The Achievements and Difficulties of the Soviet Government*, March-April 1919; *On Co-operation,* January 1923; *Better Fewer, But Better*, March 1923.

5 *C.W.*, Vol.33,p.475: *On Co-operation*, 4-6 January 1923.

6 In an article in *L'Humanité* of 20 June 1969 Claude Prévost proposed this way of "dissecting" Lenin's concept of culture which I have adopted here, because I think it valid. Prévost nevertheless seems to me not to have appreciated the possibilities of development that this "dissection" suggests: and the main reason for this, I think, is the total absence of any critical analysis which is characteristic of too many writings about Lenin.

7 *C.W.*, Vol.27, p.129: *Report on the Review of the Programme and on Changing the Name of the Party*, 8 March 1918.

8 In a passage written in 1918 Lenin makes a violent denunciation of capitalist society, as a result of the disasters caused by the imperialist war, which represents, for him, the extreme, most barbarous example of the way capitalism uses its civilisation:
"But now, in the twentieth century, side by side with

wonderful inventions, side by side with the wide application of machinery and electricity, of modern internal combustion engines in agriculture, side by side with all this we now see this same disaster of famine advancing upon the people in all European countries without exception. It would seem that despite civilisation, despite culture, the countries are once again returning to primitive savagery, are again experiencing a situation when morals deteriorate and people become brutalised in the struggle for a crust of bread." (*Speech at the 4th Conference of Trade Unions and Factory Committees of Moscow*, 27 June 1918: *C.W.*, Vol.27, pp.459-460.)

9 This "Europeanism" of Lenin's can doubtless also be linked with the thought of Russia's liberal intelligensia of the 19th century, in particular that of Herzen, Chernyshevsky and Nekrasov.

10 "Oblomovism" comes from the name, Oblomov, of the central character in the novel of the same name, by Ivan Goncharov — an embodiment of routine and inertia.

11 *C.W.*, Vol.32, pp.349-350: *The Tax in Kind*, 21 April 1921.

12 *C.W.*, Vol.33, p.462: *Pages from a Diary*, 2 January 1923: Here is an excerpt from another work which is especially explicit on this matter:
"From the point of view of the 'enlightened' (primarily, literate) European, there is not much left for us to do to induce absolutely everyone to take not a passive, but an active part in co-operative operations. Strictly speaking, there is '*only*' one thing we have left to do and that is to make our people so 'enlightened' that they understand all the advantages of everybody participating in the work of the co-operatives, and organise this participation. '*Only*' that. There are

now no other devices needed to advance socialism. But to achieve this 'only' there must be a veritable revolution — the entire people must go through a period of cultural development ... The thing now is to learn to combine the wide revolutionary range of action, the revolutionary enthusiasm which we have displayed, and displayed abundantly, and crowned with complete success — to learn to combine this with (I am almost inclined to say) the ability to be an efficient and capable trader, which is quite enough to be a good co-operator. By ability to be a trader I mean the ability to be a cultured trader. Let those Russians, or peasants, who imagine that since they trade they are good traders, get that well into their heads. This does not follow at all. They do trade, but that is far from being cultured traders. They now trade in an Asiatic manner, but to be a good trader one must trade in the European manner. They are a whole epoch behind in that." (*C.W.*, Vol.33, pp.469-470: *On Co-operation*, January 1923.)

13 *C.W.*, Vol.33, p.478: *On Revolution*, 16-17 January 1923.

14 *C.W.*, Vol. 27, p.310: *Session of the All-Russia C.E.C.*, 29 April 1918.

15 *C.W.*, Vol.20, p.24: *Critical Remarks on the National Question*, October-December 1913.

16 What is involved here is the "broad" sense of ideology, which, as a system of representation of a given social reality, is a phenomenon that is common to, and even inherent in, all human societies. At this level, what it is that disappears, or can be destroyed, is the particular *ideological form* of a given society at a certain moment in its history. In order to avoid confusion we must distinguish this "broad" sense, which does not, in itself, imply a value-judgment, from a

"narrow" sense, often used by Marx and Engels, the import of which is always pejorative. In this second sense, ideology means "occupation with thoughts as with independent entities, developing independently and subject only to their own laws" (Engels, *Ludwig Feuerbach*, in Marx and Engels, *Selected Works in Three Volumes*, Moscow, Progress, 1970, Vol.3, p.372). We could also adopt for the purpose of our analysis the definition of ideology given by Althusser in *For Marx*:

"Ideology, then, is the expression of the relation between men and their 'world', that is, the (over-determined) unity of the real relation and the imaginary relation between them and their real conditions of existence. In ideology the real relation is inevitably invested in the imaginary relation, a relation that *expresses* a *will* (conservative, conformist, reformist or revolutionary), a hope or a nostalgia, rather than describing a reality." (L. Althusser, *For Marx*, London, Penguin, 1969, pp.233-234.)

17 "Happily, the time for purely theoretical discussions, disputes over general questions, and the adoption of resolutions on principles has passed. *That stage is over: it was dealt with and settled yesterday and the day before yesterday* [My emphasis, C.C-U.]. We must march ahead, and we must realise that we are now confronted by a *practical* task, the *business* task of rapidly overcoming economic chaos, and we must do it with all our strength ..." (*C.W.*, Vol.30, p.405. See also Vol.31, pp.402 and 404.) Also this: "After we had solved the problem of the greatest political revolution in history, other problems confronted us, cultural problems, which may be called 'minor affairs.' " (*C.W..*, Vol.33, p.73).

18 In the second part of this book will be found my
     analysis of the role played, in the problematic being
     studied, by Lenin's conception of the Party.
19 *C.W.*, Vol.27, p.464: *Speech at 4th Conference of
     Moscow Trade Unions and Factory Committees*,
     27 June 1918: my emphasis, C.C-U.
20 *C.W.*, Vol.36, p.570: *Letter to I.I.Skvortsov-
     Stepanov*, 9 March 1922.
21 *C.W.*, Vol.26, p.352: *The Tasks of the Public
     Library in Leningrad*, November 1917.
22 *C.W.*, Vol.30, p.377: *Speech at 3rd All-Russia Con-
     ference of Directors of Adult Education Divisions of
     Gubernia Education Departments*, 25 February 1920
     another passage (from *C.W.*, Vol.33, p. 246) shows
     the importance ascribed by Lenin to the problem of
     electrification, and how it seems to him to be directly
     linked with the problem of culture: "The Eighth
     Congress of Soviets decreed that instruction on the
     Plan for Electrification should be compulsory in all
     educational establishments in the R.S.F.S.R., with-
     out exception. This decree, like many others, has
     remained a dead letter because of our (Bolsheviks')
     lack of culture. Now that Comrade Stepanov's
     'manual for schools' has been published we must see
     to it ... that every *uyezd* library (and later every
     volost library) obtains several copies of it and that
     every electric power station in Russia ... arranges
     popular lectures on electricity, on the electrification
     of the R.S.F.S.R. and on engineering in general ...
     It will require no little effort to do this. We are poor
     and uneducated. But that does not matter so long as
     our people realise that they must learn, and so long as
     they are willing to learn; so long as the workers and
     peasants clearly understand that they must now learn;
     not to [create] 'benefit' and produce profits for the

landowners and capitalists, but to improve *their own* conditions of life."

23 *C.W.*, Vol.26, pp.481-482: *Summing-Up Speech at 3rd All-Russia Congress of Soviets*, 18(31) January 1918.

24 *C.W.*, Vol.33, p.487: *Better Fewer, but Better*, 2 March 1923.

25 *C.W.*, Vol.27, p.412: *Speech at the First Congress of Economic Councils*, 26 May 1918.

26 *C.W.*, Vol.29, p.70: *The Achievements and Difficulties of the Soviet Government*, March-April 1919.

27 *C.W.*, Vol.29, p.24: *Session of the Petrograd Soviet*, 12 March 1919.

28 *C.W.*, Vol.31, pp.286-7: *The Tasks of the Youth Leagues*: 2 October 1920.

29 *Ibid.*

30 *C.W.*, Vol.29, p.178: *Report on the Party Programme*, 19 March 1919.

31 This idea of a straight distinction between the content of culture and the use made of it is sometimes extended by Lenin, without any attempt at theoretical justification, to the bourgeois cultural apparatus in its entirety. "Everything that bourgeois culture has created for the purpose of deceiving the people and defending the capitalists we have taken from them in order to satisfy the political needs of the workers and peasants." (*C.W.*, Vol.29, p.163: *Report of the Central Committee to the 8th Party Congress*, 18 March 1919.)

32 *C.W.*, Vol.29, p.183: *Report on the Party Programme*, 19 March 1919.

33 *C.W.*, Vol. 33, p.194: *The Role and Functions of the Trade Unions under the N.E.P.*, 12 January 1922.

34 *C.W.*, Vol. 28, p.381: *Speech at the 2nd Congress of the Economic Councils*, 25 December 1918.

35 *C.W.*, Vol.29, p.73: *The Achievements and Difficulties of the Soviet Government*, March-April 1919.

36 *C.W.*, Vol. 29, pp.180-181: *Report on the Party Programme*, 19 March 1919.

37 *C.W.*, Vol.27, p.250: *The Immediate Tasks of the Soviet Government*, March-April 1918. It seems to me very important, from every standpoint, to highlight here the attitude taken by Lenin towards this question of high salaries. It could be described as exemplarily Marxist, in that it does not try to hide the truth from the masses and does not shrink from calling a spade a spade: it is an attitude that was to disappear all too soon from official Soviet history, to give place to a veritable ideological masquerade. I therefore think fit to give this long quotation from *The Immediate Tasks of the Soviet Government*, in which we hear language that was thereafter to be long forgotten. "*Now we have to resort* [my emphasis, C.C-U.] to the old bourgeois method and to agree to pay a very high price for the 'services' of the top bourgeois experts. All those who are familiar with the subject appreciate this, but not all ponder over the significance of this measure being adopted by the proletarian state. *Clearly, this measure is a compromise, a departure from the principles of the Paris Commune and of every proletarian power* [my emphasis, C.C-U], which call for the reduction of all salaries to the level of the wages of the average worker, which urge that careerism be fought not merely in words but in deeds.

"Moreover, it is clear that this measure not only implies the cessation — in a certain field and to a certain degree — of the offensive against capital (for capital is not a sum of money, but a definite social relation): it is also *a step backward* [Lenin's own emphasis] on the part of our socialist Soviet state power, which from the very outset proclaimed and pursued the policy of reducing high salaries to the level of the wages of the average worker ... To conceal from the people the fact that the enlistment of bourgeois experts by means of extremely high salaries is a retreat from the principles of the Paris Commune would be sinking to the level of bourgeois politicians and deceiving the people. Frankly explaining how and why we took this step backward, and then publicly discussing what means are available for making up for lost time, means educating the people and learning from experience, learning together with the people how to build socialism." (*C.W.*, Vol.27, pp.248-249).

38 *C.W.*, Vol.29, p.180: *Report on the Party Programme*, 19 March 1919.

39 In his *Speech at the 3rd All-Russia Congress of Water-Transport Workers* (15 March 1920) Lenin says: "Earlier revolutions perished because the workers were unable to retain power by means of a firm dictatorship and did not realise that they could not retain power by dictatorship by force, by coercion alone; power can be maintained only by adopting the whole experience of cultured, technically-equipped progressive capitalism and by enlisting the services of all these people" (*C.W.*, Vol.30, pp.429-430).

40 *C.W.*, Vol.29, p.448: *All Out for the Fight Against Denikin!*, 3 July 1919. In an article for *Pravda* written in February 1921 (*A Single Economic Plan*), Lenin comes back to this idea in connexion with the affairs of *Goelro*, the state commission for the electrification of Russia. It is not hard to appreciate how carefully Lenin must have weighed his words,

when we know the great importance he attributed to
the fulfilment of the plan to electrify the land of the
Soviets:

"The task of the Communists inside GOELRO is to
issue fewer orders, rather, to refrain from issuing any
at all, and to be very tactful in their dealings with the
scientists and technicians (the R.C.P. programme
says: 'Most of them inevitably have strong bourgeois
habits and take the bourgeois view of things'). The
task is to learn from them and to help them to
broaden their world-view on the basis of achieve
ments in their particular field, always bearing in
mind that the engineer's way to communism is *different* from that of the underground propagandist and
the writer; he is guided along *by the evidence of his
own science*, so that the agronomist, the forestry
expert, etc., each have *their own path* to tread toward
communism. The Communist who has failed to
prove his ability to bring together and guide the work
of specialists in a spirit of modesty, going to the heart
of the matter, and studying it in detail, is a potential
menace. We have many such Communists among us,
and I would gladly swap dozens of them for one con-
scientious qualified bourgeois specialist." (*C.W.*,
Vol.32, p.144).

41 *C.W.*, Vol.29, p.70: *The Achievements and Difficulties of the Soviet Government*, March-April 1919. Or,
again: "What has to be done just now is to tackle from
every aspect the practical erection of the edifice, the
plan of which we outlined long ago, the foundations
for which we have fought for vigorously enough and
firmly enough won, the materials for which we have
adequately collected and which now — having provided it with scaffolding and put on working clothes,
which we are not afraid of dirtying with any auxiliary

materials, and strictly fulfilling the instructions of those in charge of the practical work — we must build and build and build." (*C.W.*, Vol.27, p.214.)

42 *C.W.*, Vol.29, pp.156-157: my emphasis, C.C-U: *Report of the Central Committee to the 8th Party Congress*, 18 March 1919.

43 *C.W.*, Vol.30, p.430: *Speech at 3rd All-Russia Congress of Water Transport Workers*, 15 March 1920.

44 *C.W.*, Vol.28, pp.214-215: *Speech at Moscow Party Workers' Meeting*, 27 November 1918.

45 *C.W.*, Vol.31, p.288: *The Tasks of the Youth Leagues*, 2 October 1920.

46 *C.W.*, Vol.31, p.317: *On Proletarian Culture*, 8 October 1920: my emphasis, C.C-U.

47 *C.W.*, Vol.42, p.217: *Rough Draft of a Resolution on Proletarian Culture*, 9 October 1920: my emphasis, C.C-U.

48 "We do not regard Marx's theory as something completed and inviolable; on the contrary, we are convinced that it has only laid the foundation stone of the science which socialists *must* develop in all directions if they wish to keep pace with life. We think that an *independent* elaboration of Marx's theory is especially essential for Russian socialists; for this theory provides only general *guiding* principles, which, *in particular*, are applied in England differently than [*sic*] in France, in France differently than [*sic*] in Germany, and in Germany differently than [*sic*] in Russia" (*C.W.*, Vol.4, pp.211-212).

49 At first circumscribed by the determining reality of a revolution in progress, the far-reaching consequences of this conception did not make themselves felt until later, in the services that it rendered, when taken literally and separated from Lenin's living practice, to the policy of bringing to heel the masses and the

"proletarian" state, in an all-round way, at the beginning of the 1930s.

50 " 'The key feature of the moment' = (the link in the chain) + the gap between the grandeur of the tasks imposed and our *poverty*, not only material but also *cultural*" (*C.W.*, Vol.36, p.574). I mean here "the weakest link" specific to the Russian revolution, in so far as (a point already mentioned) this problem would not exist, according to Lenin, for any of the advanced countries. The other big problem, not unconnected with the one being discussed, was due to the circumstance that the Russian Revolution had not proved to be what its leaders, and Communists throughout the world, had long hoped it would be, namely, the signal for "the revolution on the march". Actually, any country whatsoever, even the most advanced, such as the U.S.A., would find itself faced with this same problem if its revolution turned out, like the Russian Revolution, to be an isolated event in the world. This problem would be of the same order, and so not specific to any particular country, even though the form in which it presented itself would doubtless differ from one country to another.

51 Marx and Engels, *Collected Works*, English edition, Vol.5, London, Lawrence and Wishart, 1976, p.40.

52 Marx, *The Civil War in France*, in Marx and Engels, *Selected Works in Three Volumes*, *op.cit.*, Vol.2 (1969) p.217.

53 A contraction of the Russian expression *proletarskaya kultura*, "proletarian culture".

54 Comparison between the theses of *Proletkult* and those of the Chinese Revolution is obviously called for, their similarity is so striking. I think it is all the more interesting to stress this fact because it is usually

quite unknown or else deliberately passed over in silence. On the basis of the whole analysis given in this first part of the book, I think I am justified in suggesting that the principal theses of the Great Chinese Cultural Revolution, even after the "rectification" campaigns, do *not* belong to the lineage of Lenin's ideas on the question, despite the plentiful references to Lenin to be met with in the Chinese documents. To make this point, since the book's scope does not permit an exhaustive analysis of the problem, I shall put side by side, for the cases that provide the best examples, the *Proletkult* theses discussed and the documents of the Chinese Cultural Revolution.

55 In *The Great Socialist Cultural Revolution in China*: Vol.3, published in Peking by the Foreign Languages Press in 1966, we read (p.4): "The proletarian cultural revolution is aimed not only at demolishing all the old ideology and culture and all the old customs and habits which, fostered by the exploiting classes, have poisoned the minds of the people for thousands of years, but also at creating and fostering among the masses an entirely new ideology and culture and entirely new customs and habits — those of the proletariat". Again, in Vol.I of the same publication, which also appeared in 1966, on page 25: "The question of which will win out in the ideological sphere is far from settled. We must pay great attention to the reaction of the superstructure on the economic base and to the class struggle in the ideological sphere. The victory of the socialist revolution on the economic and political fronts cannot be consolidated without the victory of the socialist revolution in the ideological sphere".

56 Pletnev, *On the Ideological Front*, published in

Pravda, 27 September 1922, and reprinted, with Lenin's notes, in the symposium *Voprosy Kultury pri diktature proletariata* (Problems of culture under the dictatorship of the proletariat), Moscow, 1925. [Pletnev's article and Lenin's notes on it are included in the collection of Lenin's writings. *O literature i iskusstve* (On literature and art), 2nd edition, Moscow, 1960, pp.567-569: *Trans.*]

I reproduce below the declaration of the First All-Russia Conference of *Proletkult*, which enables one to form an overall idea of this organisation's views, in the field of literature as in other fields.

"The First All-Russia Conference of Proletarian Culture Organisations, considering:

"(1) That the cultural movement among the proletariat should have an independent place alongside the political and economic movement,

"(2) That its task consists in elaborating a proletarian culture which, with the destruction of society's division into classes, will become common to all mankind.

"(3) That the organisation of this new culture must be based upon social labour and comradely collaboration.

"Resolves:

"(1) The proletariat, in order to carry out the task assigned to it, must assimilate everything in previously-existing culture that bears the imprint of common humanity.

"(2) It must undertake this assimilation in a critical way, and recast the material in the crucible of its own class-consciousness.

"(3) Proletarian culture must be revolutionary-socialist in character, so that the proletariat may be able to equip itself with fresh knowledge, organise its feelings by means of the new art, and transform its way of life in a new, truly proletarian, that is, collectivist spirit.

"(4) In its work in creating the new culture the proletariat must show the greatest class energy and independence, while using, so far as this is possible, the help of revolutionary-socialist intellectuals.

"(5) In laying the foundations of this new form of the working class movement, *Proletkult*, and defending its independence from the standpoint of organisation, so that proletarian creativity of a strictly class character may develop to the fullest extent, the Conference considers that the institutions of government, both central and local, ought to promote the movement by every means available, so as to consolidate the conquests of the literary revolution, to vanquish the bourgeoisie not only materially but also spiritually, and to build all the sooner the new edifice of the socialist society of the future." (*Proletarskaya Kultura* No.5, November 1918, p.31. Reprinted in V.Polonsky, *Ocherki literaturnogo dvizhenii revolyusionnogo epokhi* (Sketches of the literary movement of the revolutionary epoch), Moscow, 1929, p.252, note 32.)

57 It is, basically, this reduction of all manifestations of culture to its ideological substructure that forms the line of demarcation between Lenin's point of view, on the one hand, and the line of *Proletkult* and the Chinese Cultural Revolution, on the other, in determining the relation between culture and revolution and acting in accordance with this analysis. In contrast to Lenin, the other two always approach the problematic from the angle of the expression of a class ideology, a class-ideological function, either bourgeois or proletarian. This is why, in their

documents, the expressions "ideological domain" (or "ideological front") and "cultural domain" are treated as being purely and simply interchangeable.

58 Compare, in the Chinese documents:

"The struggle to foster what is proletarian and liquidate what is bourgeois on the cultural front is an important aspect of the class struggle between the proletariat and the bourgeoisie, between the socialist road and the capitalist road, and between proletarian ideology and bourgeois ideology ... Since the remnant forces of the bourgeoisie in our country are still fairly large, since there are still a fairly large number of bourgeois intellectuals, since the influence of bourgeois ideology is still fairly strong ... we shall find it difficult to see the struggle that is taking place and may fall victim to the sugar-coated bullets of the bourgeoisie or we may even lose our positions ..." (*The Great Socialist Cultural Revolution in China*, Vol.I, pp.1-2).

59 *Voprosy kultury ...*, *op.cit.*, p.13.

60 *Ibid.*, p.16.

61 But this is held to be true only of such branches as science and technology, that is, those branches which are more or less closely connected with *production* — which cannot be halted while waiting for it to become "proletarian". In the field of art, on the other hand, *Proletkult* often fell into the excesses of witch-hunting.

62 *Voprosy kultury ...*, *op.cit.*, pp.9-10.

63 The question of the "specialists" enables us to measure fully the distance between Lenin's ideas and those of the Chinese Cultural Revolution. To this end it is sufficient to compare, for instance, Lenin's article on the work of *Goelro* (note 42) and the following passage, from *The Great Socialist Cultural*

Revolution, Vol.I, p.39: "In demanding that we recognise the 'great significance' of the 'miscellaneous scholars' for the 'work of leadership', Teng To was, in effect, demanding that the Party open the door to those 'miscellaneous scholars' who had taken the capitalist road and allow them to lead in 'all kinds of work of leadership' and in 'scientific research work' — in other words, in the academic and ideological fields — and so to prepare public opinion for the restoration of capitalism."

64 Bukharin, speech at the meeting of 9 May 1924, convened by the Press Department of the Central Committee of the Party, to discuss Party policy in the sphere of literature, included in *Voprosy kultury pri diktature proletariata, op.cit.* It should be mentioned that Bukharin, though known in the West mainly for his economic writings, was also greatly interested in problems of culture and its relation to the revolution and the Party. As in most such cases, his physical murder was accompanied by an intellectual one: his writings have been little translated and are to a large extent unappreciated. Yet his attitude on the problem that interests us here seems, from the little we know about it, to be a very interesting one. It lies half-way, so to speak, between the extremes of Lenin and *Proletkult*, raising the question of the need for an intrinsic specificity in the culture of socialist society while at the same time repudiating a certain intellectual "reign of terror" which can be seen as being more or less implicit in the theses of *Proletkult*.

65 This desire was translated in practice into a sectarian and exclusive attitude towards all creativity or research, artistic or scientific, that did not swear by *Proletkult*, the only organisation considered as authorised to issue certificates testifying that one was

a genuine representative of proletarian culture.

66 *C.W.*, Vol.42, p.217 (9 October 1920).

67 *C.W.*, Vol.31, p.284 (*The Tasks of the Youth Leagues*, 2 October 1920), and Vol.33, p.230 (*On the Significance of Militant Materialism*, 12 March 1922.)

68 *C.W.*, Vol.33, p.227: *On the Significance of Militant Materialism*, 12 March 1922.

Part Two

WHAT DOMINATES THIS POINT OF VIEW

Lenin's point of view on the problematic of "culture and revolution" is dominated by a series of assumptions which condition the entire elaboration of his thought on this theme, and in relation to which we need to keep in mind that his ideas mainly took shape *after* the conquest of power, that is, parallel with the actual process of the revolution. These assumptions remain merely implicit, as a rule, in the passages we have examined up to now, and which are, as has been said, Lenin's principal writings on the problem. Explicit expression of them is therefore to be sought "elsewhere", in other passages which do not seem, at first sight, to possess any determining links with the point of view that has been analysed. We need, consequently, to consider what these *a-priori* notions, or more precisely, these theoretical schemata, are to which Lenin remains prisoner, what their connexion is with our present problematic, and what they imply for both the theory and the praxis of the proletarian revolution.

I. *The "subject" of the revolution*

1. THE PROLETARIAT AND THE PARTY OF THE PROLETARIAT

Lenin never claims to be questioning the thesis propounded on several occasions by Marx and Engels, in various of their writings, according to which the proletariat is, first and foremost, the destined "subject" of the revolution, the idea expressed in the slogan of the International: "The emancipation of the workers must be the task of the workers themselves". However, although he does not challenge this principle, Lenin departs a long way from the Marxian schema as soon as he takes up the question of how the principle is to be translated into reality and how it can be applied to this reality — in other words, as soon as he analyses the actual situation of the working class and notes the distance separating the historical class, invested with the liberating mission of bringing about "the overthrow of the capitalist mode of production and final abolition of all classes",[1] and the concrete class, incapable *in itself* of accomplishing this mission, which nevertheless remains unrealisable without it. Lenin does indeed consider that there is such a distance. What follows, logically, is that the gap must be filled, that there must be mediation, in the form of the party of the proletariat, the *locus* and instrument of the union between the historical class and the class as it concretely exists. Lenin thus initiates, in practical activity, a certain theory of the proletarian party which is not to be found in the thinkers to whose authority this theory appeals, namely, Marx and Engels. My concern here is not to contrast Lenin with Marx and Engels but to see what Lenin introduced that was new and strictly "Leninist", into the theory on which he relied, and what incidence this original contribution had on the matter we are studying here.

It is in *What Is To Be Done?*, written in 1902 — that is, long before the concrete experience of a proletarian revolution — that Lenin sets forth the essence of his analysis of the situation of the working class, and from this deduces the need for a Party *external to the class* and yet embodying its interests, both historical and immediate, and taking responsibility for its revolutionary mission.

We do not find in Marx and Engels any systematic

theoretical discussion of the proletarian party. For them the form it may take must inevitably vary, depending on the contextual facts. In any case, they never look upon it otherwise than as an essentially practical instrument, temporary, and necessarily flexible if it is to be effective. The party can only be a momentary expression of and a supplementary factor in the struggle waged by the proletariat, never a substitute for the latter: "The 'League', like the *Société des Saisons* in Paris and like a hundred other societies, was only an episode in the history of the Party, which is growing everywhere spontaneously from the soil of modern society ... By 'Party' I mean the Party in the broad historical sense".[2]

No higher instance (leader or Party), with claims to charisma, is capable of replacing this maturation of the proletariat's consciousness which is constituted by its own practice of the class struggle. For it is in struggle, *in practice*, that the proletariat, this class "completely shut off from all self-activity", acquires consciousness of itself and becomes transformed from a class "in itself" into a class "for itself". It is in practice that the proletarians become aware that they "are in a position to achieve a complete and no longer restricted self-activity, which consists in the appropriation of a totality of productive forces and in the development of a totality of capacities entailed by this".[3]

It is thus in practice that the proletariat's consciousness is forged, consciousness of the necessity of its revolution, consciousness that serves, in turn, to enrich and clarify practice. The process is therefore a dialectical one at every stage, as is correctly stressed in the third of Marx's *Theses on Feuerbach*: "The coincidence of the changing of circumstances and of human activity or self-change can be conceived and rationally understood only as *revolutionary practice*".[4]

No doubt the intellectuals (inevitably of bourgeois origin) who join the revolutionary movement make a contribution, through the theory they work out, to the proletariat's development of consciousness, but they can never be the creators of this consciousness. And it is on this fundamental question — *how* does the concrete working class become conscious of its "objective social being"? — that the cleavage occurs between Lenin's theory and the Marxian schema I have just outlined. For Lenin, the proletarians, bogged down in their situation as victims of exploitation, in their struggle restricted to demands for betterment of their conditions of life and work, uneducated and excluded by the capitalist system from any access to culture — this concrete working class cannot by itself raise its eyes above the limited horizon of the dichotomy of employers and wage-earners, to attain that *knowledge* of society as a whole which alone makes it possible to understand (and act upon) the connexions linking the regime of exploitation and the political structure of the capitalist state. This is why, according to Lenin, "the working class is able, by its own efforts alone, to develop only trade-union consciousness", that is to say, the reformism of a struggle that is purely economic, and incapable by its very nature of smashing the framework of bourgeois production-relations. In other words, left to itself, the working class can only keep within the rules of the game dictated by the commodity-relations of bourgeois society; it can only sell itself at a higher price, while thereby sinking, more surely even than before, into an increased state of dependence: "The *spontaneous* development of the working-class movement leads to its subordination to bourgeois ideology ... for the spontaneous working-class movement is trade-unionism, is *Nur-Gewerkschaftlerei*, and trade-unionism means the

ideological enslavement of the workers by the bourgeoisie".[5]

   Actually, the proletariat is unable, on its own, to
determine itself as the subject of the revolutionary
process. It is therefore not from the proletariat's practice
that its consciousness as a class "for itself" can come, but
only *from outside*. The working class has to be educated
and elevated to knowledge of its identity as a revolutionary class and of the conditions for its own emancipation:

   "Class political consciousness can be brought to the
   workers *only from without*, that is, only from outside
   the economic struggle, from outside the sphere of
   relations between workers and employers. The
   sphere from which alone it is possible to obtain this
   knowledge is the sphere of relationships of *all* classes
   and strata to the state and the government, the
   sphere of the interrelations between *all* classes".[6]

Now, this knowledge is possessed by the bourgeois
intellectuals and can be *transmitted* to the working class
only through them. At this vital stage of his analysis
Lenin supports his argument not with a passage from
Marx or Engels, as he undoubtedly would not have failed
to do if such a passage had been available, but with a
quotation from Kautsky, whose ideas in this connexion he
describes as "profoundly just and important". Despite its
length, I shall here reproduce this passage in full, since it
constitutes the only theoretical "backing" that Lenin
provides:

"Many of our revisionist critics believe that Marx asserted that economic development and the class struggle create not only the conditions for socialist production but also, and directly, the *consciousness* [Kautsky's italics] of its necessity ... But this is absolutely untrue. Of course, socialism, as a doctrine, has its roots in modern economic relationships, just as the class struggle of the proletariat has, and, like the latter, emerges from the struggle against the capitalist-created poverty and misery of the masses. But socialism and the class struggle arise side by side and not one out of the other: each arises under different conditions. Modern socialist consciousness can arise only on the basis of profound scientific knowledge. Indeed, modern economic science is as much a condition for socialist production as, say, modern technology, and the proletariat can create neither the one nor the other, no matter how much it may desire to do so ... The vehicle of science is not the proletariat, but the *bourgeois intelligentsia* [Kautsky's italics]; it was in the minds of individual members of this stratum that modern socialism originated, and it was they who communicated it to the more intellectually developed proletarians who, in their turn, introduce it into the proletarian class struggle where conditions allow that to be done. Thus, socialist consciousness is something intro duced into the proletarian class struggle from without and not something that arose within it spontaneously ... The task of Social-Democracy is to imbue the proletariat [literally: saturate the proletariat] with the *consciousness* of its position and the consciousness of its task' ".[7]

From this organic incapacity of the proletariat to raise itself to attain knowledge and so, for Lenin, consciousness of itself as agent of the revolutionary process, it follows inevitably that the proletariat cannot, either, work out the plan for the revolution; which revolution nevertheless cannot be achieved without its participation. Hence the need for a vanguard — depository of the revolutionary consciousness of the historical class and of scientific knowledge of its potentialities, bearer of the political plan, external to the concrete class, its definition being that of its function: to make the revolution. This vanguard, the Party, thus realises, in the persons of its "professional revolution-aries", its "full-timers" in the service of the revolution, the symbiosis of the social being of the proletariat and its consciousness, and embodies the reconciled identity of the historical class and the class as a concrete reality.

If one still needs convincing of the fundamental revision contained in the analysis given in *What Is To Be Done?*, although this is presented as a strictly Marxian exegesis, it is enough to refer, for example, to the passage in *The German Ideology* in which Marx and Engels set forth what amounts to a summary of their conception of history:

"In the development of productive forces there comes a stage when productive forces and means of intercourse are brought into being which, under the existing relations, can only cause mischief ...; and connected with this a class is called forth which has to bear all the burdens of society without enjoying its advantages, which is ousted from society and forced into the sharpest contradiction to all other classes; a class which forms the majority of all

members of society, and *from which emanates the
consciousness of the necessity of a fundamental
revolution, the communist consciousness, which
may, of course, arise among the other classes too*
through the contemplation of the situation of this
class".[8]

This passage shows clearly, by contrast, the idealistic bias
of the Leninist revision, which makes class-consciousness
dependent necessarily on socialist theory, and the latter a
pure product of *culture*. For Lenin, the question is finally
settled: the proletarians are not "cultured", and so they
cannot be "conscious". This is the diametrical opposite of
Marx's third thesis on Feuerbach: for Lenin *consciousness
comes from knowledge*, and not from practice, from the
dialectical relation between a person and his social world.
In other words, it is no longer social being that
determines consciousness, but the reverse, and there is
even "derivation of consciousness from consciousness",
with the consciousness of the proletariat becoming "the
product of the consciousness of intellectuals miraculously
detached from their social being and abstracted from
their class".[9] It seems to me that one is justified in
thinking that these ideas of Lenin's are more Hegelian
than Marxian: the mediation between the proletariat and
its consciousness is effected by the socialist intellectuals,
elevated, as K. Papaioannou has observed, after the
fashion of the functionaries of Hegel's State, into a sort of
universal class possessed of the science of society as a
whole ("the interest of the Idea") — "an interest of which
these members of civil society are as such unconscious".[10]
    It is interesting to note the analogy, not to say the
identity, between the definitions given by Lenin of

of proletarian culture, on the one hand (see p.26), and, on the other, of "the theoretical doctrine of social-democracy", that is, the socialist doctrine, of which he says that it arose, as "the history of all countries shows", "altogether independently of the spontaneous growth of the working-class movement; it arose *as a natural and inevitable outcome of the development of thought* among the revolutionary socialist intelligentsia".[11] This parallel enables us to perceive the high degree of coherence in Lenin's thought. Everything that was set forth in the first part of this book, and especially Lenin's conception of culture-as-knowledge and of the type of cultural revolution it presumes, its relation to the masses, the role of the intellectuals, and so on, is rigorously and logically linked with Lenin's conception of the relation between the Party and the class, the dialectic of which tends, with him, to replace the Marxian dialectic of class and society. It is a coherence of thought which, moreover, shuts the proletarian up in a sort of "nursery-school" of history where, whichever way he turns, he is always the "ignorant" pupil of some educator or other, whom it is hard to perceive how he will ever cease to need. It is, in fact, inevitable that the role with which Lenin endows the "enlightened" vanguard acquires a determining didactic dimension, just as with Marx, but in the manner of a photographic negative. For Marx the self-emancipation of the proletariat is inseparable from its *self-education*, to which the contribution made by the correct knowledge of a possible "teacher" is much less, in the long run, so far as the revolution is concerned, than that which results from the mistakes, even the repeated mistakes, made by the "pupil". In this sense, and in the light of what eventually became of all the hopes and all the illusions of the October Revolution, Rosa Luxemburg's warning to the Bolsheviks takes on the value of a prophecy:

> "The nimble acrobat ['his majesty the central
> committee'] fails to see that the true subject to whom
> [the] role of director falls is the collective ego of the
> working class, which insists on its right to make its
> own mistakes and to learn the historical dialectic
> by itself. Finally, we must frankly admit to our-
> selves that errors made by a truly revolutionary
> labour movement are historically infinitely more
> fruitful and more valuable than the infallibility of
> the best of all possible 'central committees".[12]

With the taking of power in October 1917 the Leninist
conception of the Party and the relations between Party
and class could not fail to mediatise the process of the
"taking-over" by the masses of the machinery of state and
the means of production, and this in turn was bound to
determine the type of social relations that were to arise
from it.

2. THE PROLETARIAT AND THE PROLETARIAN STATE

Lenin was led to modify his views after having seen at
work, first in 1905 and then in 1917, the proletariat
which, "left to its own efforts" did not at all tend to "take
refuge under the wing of the bourgeoisie". The
revolutionary crisis enabled Lenin, in fact, to see clearly
the action of a proletariat which had broken away from
the meshes of the productive-relations that paralysed it,
and as a result of this, the union, now begun at last, in
the form of the Soviets, between the "historical" class and
the class as a concrete reality. Most of Lenin's writings in
this exceptional period sound a note that was thereafter

to become rarer and rarer — they are dominated by
confidence in the creative capacities of the masses, who
had not been to "the despicable school of the bourgeoisie", and in the political decisions of the masses,
whatever these might be.[13]

> "Comrades, working people! Remember that now
> *you yourselves* are at the helm of the state. No one
> will help you if you yourselves do not unite and take
> into *your* hands *all affairs* of the state. *Your* Soviets
> are from now on the organs of state authority, legis-
> lative bodies with full powers. Rally round your
> Soviets. Strengthen them. Get on with the job your-
> selves; begin right at the bottom, do not wait for
> anyone."[14]

The slogan put forward on Lenin's initiative, "All power
to the Soviets!", expressed his profound conviction that
the great moment had come when the masses would force
their way to the forefront of history's stage. "A phase of
transparency" began; but this gave rise at once to "the
major problem of socialism, which consists in preserving
this political transparency, transferring it from the
insurrection to the government, so that it may be
introduced subsequently into all social and economic
spheres, through taking full possession of the state and of
every institution".[15] Once the euphoria of victory had
passed and once the historical stage had been reached
when it was necessary to get down in a practical way to
the task of peacefully building a new life, Lenin saw the
"vicious circle" of Asiatic backwardness closing once
more. That the proletariat, no less "ignorant" than
before, had shown proof of its class-consciousness does

not appear to have caused Lenin to reconsider the fundamental ideas he had set out in *What Is To Be Done?*[16] On the contrary, as he progressed in experience of power, Lenin was confirmed in *these* ideas, and was led to revise, in practice, some of the ideas regarding the way the proletarian state should be run that he had expressed in *The State and Revolution*, where he had looked forward to the withering away in the near future of every form of officialdom, with administrative tasks being undertaken by everyone in turn and thereby ceasing to be the special activity of particular persons.[17] For the same lack of culture in the proletariat and the masses which makes the Party's intervention indispensable if they are to attain class-consciousness gives rise at the same time to the necessity for mediation by the Party in the direct management of a machine which, moreover, still has to be created.

> "What elements have we for building this machine? Only two. First, the workers who are absorbed in the struggle for socialism. These elements are not sufficiently educated. They would like to build a better machine for us, but they don't know how. They cannot build one. They have not yet developed the culture required for this: and it is culture that is required ... Secondly, we have elements of knowledge, education and training, but they are ridiculously inadequate compared with all other countries."[18]

Since the system has got to function without waiting until the proletariat has attained "the level of culture required", but also so as not to betray the interests of the proletariat, which has made the system possible, it is for the Party, quite "naturally", to assume the task of running the state and all the institutions, until the time comes when the masses can take in hand the immediate management of their affairs.

"But the dictatorship of the proletariat cannot be exercised through an organisation embracing the whole of that class, because *in all capitalist countries* (and not only over here, in one of the most backward) the proletariat is still so divided, so degraded, and so corrupted in parts ... that an organisation taking in the whole proletariat cannot *directly* exercise proletarian dictatorship. It can be exercised only by a vanguard that has absorbed the revolutionary energy of the class."[19]

Now, while the state, even the proletarian state, sets limits by its mere existence to the transparency of social relations, limits which the revolution has to push back until they disappear with the final extinction of the state, the mediation exercised by the Party comes in, to add to this opacity a veil that is to prove all the more difficult to tear away because it will be increasingly unwilling to admit that that is just what it is.

Postulated as being necessary for the taking over of the state by the masses, the Party's mediation is in turn conditioned by Lenin's analysis of the modern state, that is, the state as it exists in advanced capitalist societies, and of the type of managerial qualities that this requires. Here, too, Lenin concludes, and this in the first hours of the revolution, it is necessary to utilise a certain bourgeois heritage which is indispensable for the building of socialism — making a clear-cut distinction between the state as political power and the state as administration, between an apparatus that carries out a class-ideological function and an apparatus of a technical order, so to speak, the class nature of which is not inherent but "added", being determined by that of the first-mentioned apparatus.

"In addition to the chiefly 'oppressive' apparatus — the standing army, the policy and the bureaucracy — the modern state possesses an apparatus which has extremely close connexions with the banks and syndicates, an apparatus which performs an enormous amount of accounting and registration work, if it may be expressed this way. This apparatus must not, and should not be smashed. It must be wrested from the control of the capitalists; the capitalists and the wires they pull must be *cut off, lopped off, chopped away from* this apparatus; it must be *subordinated* to the proletarian soviets; it must be expanded, made more comprehensive and nationwide. And this *can* be done by utilising the achievements already made by large-scale capitalism ... Capitalism has created an accounting *apparatus* in the shape of the banks, syndicates, postal services, consumers' societies and office employees' unions. *Without big banks socialism would be impossible.* The big banks are the 'state apparatus' which need to bring about socialism, and which we *take readymade* from capitalism: our task here is to *lop off* what *capitalistically mutilates* [see note — Trans.] this excellent apparatus, to make it *even bigger,* even more democratic, even more comprehensive. Quantity will be transformed into quality."[20]

After carrying out this surgical operation all that remains to be done, once this healthy body, the "technical" apparatus, has been separated off, is to "workerise" it by gradually bringing the masses into it.[21] But this "workerisation" cannot be accomplished at once, for the valuable services rendered by this administrative apparatus are due precisely to its high technical quality, which necessitates special abilities — first and foremost, competence, the fruit of long experience and advanced culture[22] — abilities that the Soviet power lacks.

"What we lack most is culture, administrative ability. Economically and politically NEP makes it fully possible for us to lay the foundations of socialist economy. It is 'only' a matter of the cultural forces of the proletariat and of its vanguard."[23]

We therefore have, once more, to take the path to the only school in which this knowledge is to be had, namely, the school of the bourgeoisie, and, once more, to utilise the services of the only individuals who can put this knowledge into application at once, namely, the bourgeois administrator-technicians.

"... I refer you to the bourgeoisie. Whom we shall learn from, if not the bourgeoisie? How did they manage? They managed as a class when [the bourgeoisie] was the ruler, but didn't it appoint managers? We haven't yet caught up with them in their degree of development. They knew how to rule as a class, and to manage through anyone you please individually, entirely in their own interests; at the

top they had a small collegium and they didn't discuss basic principles and didn't write such resolutions. They had all power in their hands, and
regarded as competent the one who knew his job.
The workers have not yet reached that point, and
in order to win we must give up our old prejudices.
*The rule of the working class is reflected in the con-
stitution, the [system of] ownership and in the fact
that it is we who are running things, while management is quite another matter, it is a question of
skill, a question of experience.* The bourgeoisie
understood this perfectly, but we have not yet
realised it. Let's get down to learning."[24]

In other places too Lenin reiterates that the proletariat
holds, through the Party, all the political power it needs,
but that this power is meaningless if it is not translated
into practice, that is, if it does not also ensure that it also
possesses the power of knowledge. In short, political
power is dependent on the power of knowledge, and
culture becomes the point of anchorage of the problematic of proletarian power. "The state apparatus in general:
bad beyond description; lower than the bourgeois level of
culture; ... it is a question of culture in general, and it
will take years to raise it."[25]

At this level the problem affects not only the masses
in general but also, and especially, since it is through
them that the state is directly run, the Communists who
lead the masses. These Communists, says Lenin, are no
better qualified than the masses to manage, and so to
dominate, the huge machine that is a modern state.
Lenin concludes that it is from this want of knowledge
that the condition of bureaucratic plethora arises, in

which the state, and through it the power of the masses, is
in danger of getting bogged down.

"And here we must squarely put the question:
wherein lies our strength and what do we lack? *We
have quite enough political power* ... The main
economic power is in our hands ... The economic
power in the hands of the proletarian state of Russia
is quite adequate to ensure the transition to communism. *What then is lacking? Obviously what is
lacking is culture among the stratum of the Communists who perform the administrative functions.* If we
take Moscow with its 4,700 Communists in responsible positions, and if we take that huge bureaucratic
machine, that gigantic heap, we must ask: who is
directing whom? I doubt very much whether it can
truthfully be said that the Communists are directing
that heap. *To tell the truth, they are not directing,
they are being directed* ... Will the responsible
Communists of the R.S.F.S.R. and of the Russian
Communist Party realise that they cannot adminis-
ter; that they only imagine they are directing, but
are, actually, being directed? If they realise this they
will learn, of course; for this business can be learnt.
But one must study hard to learn it, and our people
are not doing this. They scatter orders and decrees
right and left, but the result is quite different from
what they want."[26]

All the premises are thus laid down for the inexorable
launching of a system of delegation of powers, at all
levels, the natural tendency of which will be to turn into
"substitution" pure and simple, with the masses

themselves necessarily excluded from power.[27] When, in the last years of his life, Lenin suddenly becomes aware of how far this harmful process has gone — in total contrast to the result expected — it is not in a modification or correction of the structures that he sees the solution, as one might have expected from a Marxist approach, but in men. "1922: The *essential* is not in institutions, not in reorganisations, not in new decrees, but in the *selection of personnel* and in *checking performance*."[28]

He thus arrives at a conception of state administration in which the élitist element, once it has been freed from the effective functioning of the mechanisms of control from below (to the withering-away of which it contributes to no small extent), will be more and more accentuated, until it finally imposes itself as something natural and legitimate, and not as a mere palliative for a situation of compelling necessity, which was how, at bottom, Lenin looked upon it. And yet Lenin's intention, undeniably guided by genuine concern to serve the interests of the masses, could not alter this process at all. It turned out, in reality, that the "solution" he put forward was no solution, precisely in so far as it sought merely to serve the end in view. Undoubtedly, Lenin's basic mistake at this crucial moment was to have opted for a policy concerned with the leaders rather than with the masses, to have underestimated, by not promoting it, the sole factor which, in my opinion, could have broken out of the vicious circle of that process, fatal to the revolution, which had begun, of political and social asphyxia — the sole factor that could have restored the revolutionary dynamic: the initiative of the masses, the vital condition for which, *sine qua non*, has always been, as the entire history of the class struggle has shown, the broadest proletarian democracy. As Lenin expressed it, this "solution" of his makes it possible, whether or not he so intended, to eliminate all real intervention by the masses in the conduct of their own affairs, since their activity remains subordinate, *de facto*, to a higher authority which, in the last analysis, itself regulates the mechanisms whereby it is controlled. The first consequence, one that is fatal for the revolution, of this "solution" is that the guarantee of the proletarian content of the state is shifted from the objective sphere — the type of social relations that may or may not be created — to the subjective (and so, by definition, uncertain) sphere of the political and moral integrity of a stratum of leaders.

> "If we do not close our eyes to reality we must admit that at the present time the proletarian policy of the Party is not determined by the character of its membership but by *the enormous undivided prestige enjoyed by the small group which might be called the Old Guard of the Party*. A slight conflict within this group will be enough, if not to destroy this prestige, at all events to weaken the group *to such a degree as to rob it of its power to determine policy*."[29]

The second consequence, no less baneful, regardless of the wishes of Lenin and the Bolshevik leaders, was to open a royal road for what Christian Rakovsky was to call, in 1928, "the occupational hazards of power", in which, following an implacable logic, the differentiation between the leaders and the led "is at first functional but afterwards becomes social".[30]

II. *The theoretical model: industrial society.*

As has been mentioned above, a second assumption places Lenin's point of view within a predetermined framework which narrowly circumscribes all his thinking about the problematic being considered. Lenin — and, generally speaking, the whole leadership of the Bolshevik Party — takes over, without first subjecting it to critical analysis, the schema offered by the Second International and, in particular, by its most eminent representative, Karl Kautsky, as being a rigorous exegesis of the thought of Marx and Engels. This schema tends to treat the type of industrial production found in advanced Western societies as the only possible reference-model for the building of socialist society.

Lenin starts from one of the fundamental components of the conception of history worked out by Marx and Engels: the "absolutely necessary practical premise" for a proletarian revolution to take place is a high level of development of the existing productive forces, for, they say, "without it, privation, want, is merely made general", which means falling back into compelling necessity, and "all the old filthy business" being restored.[31] This is why Lenin can state that productivity is, in the socialist society under construction, both the cornerstone and the touchstone to which everything else must be subordinated. Trotsky is quite in line with Lenin's thinking when he writes: "The growth of civilisation is measured by the productivity of human labour, and each new form of social relations must pass through a test on such lines".[32] Lenin thus arrives, quickly, at a conclusion the practical validity, and thereby the force, of which lies in the fact that it is empirically observable and verified: the existing type of society which has made possible an unprecedented development of the productive forces, an unheard-of growth in productivity, is none other than industrial society, based upon "large-scale machine industry". This is then identified in his mind with the "absolutely necessary practical premise" of which Marx and Engels speak, and it becomes the material pre-condition for socialism, in relation to the requirements of which not only must the entire economic organisation of the new order be constituted, but also its entire political and social organisation.

> "Socialism owes its origin to large-scale machine industry. If the masses of the working people, in introducing socialism, prove incapable of adapting their institutions to the way that large-scale industry should work, then there can be no question of introducing socialism."[33]

Now, historically, large-scale machine industry first appeared and developed under the capitalist mode of production-relations, which have marked it with a particular class character. Here we come again upon the same reasoning that Lenin implicitly engages in in the passage quoted on p.16. Large-scale industry, with the high level of scientific and technical development which it presumes, contains potentialities that are without any ideological value of their own: this ideological value is not determined spontaneously on the terrain specific to them, of the nature of the political and social interests that put them to service. This is why large-scale machine industry can, depending on the political action that conditions it, lead equally well to barbarity of an imperialistic war or to the establishment of a socialist society, to the destruction of all civilisation or to the supreme flowering of all human culture. A different political regime — a proletarian one, in fact — is all that is needed for industrial civilisation to continue to be what it is, above all, in Lenin's eyes, namely, the *locus, par excellence* of culture.

> "We must ... begin everywhere to build up our state on the basis of large-scale, machine-industry methods, *so as to make our country a cultured country,* and *by a correct socialist struggle* get out of the quagmire in which the countries of world capitalism and imperialism are at present submerged."[34]

This type of industrialisation is therefore necessarily the first-priority objective of the proletarian state, and this alone will enable it to attain the high level of productivity that it must have in order to survive. Since he adopts as it stands, *without any critical detachment,* the large-scale industry developed by capitalism as the basis *sine qua non* of Soviet construction, it is quite logical that Lenin then proceeds, naturally, to make the following assumption: the *necessary* and *sufficient* condition for ensuring the final victory of the process of socialist industrialisation and construction is to adopt the type of productivity which is seen in advanced capitalist societies, and, consequently, the type of social organisation of labour that it implies, and to develop these in a socialist way. We find concrete, and very striking, expression of these ideas in Lenin's description of the German state as the example to be followed in building socialism, the model *par excellence* of the type of economic and social organisation towards which the proletarian state and socialist production should strive with all their strength.

"To make things even clearer, let us first of all take the most concrete example of state capitalism. Everybody knows what this example is. It is Germany. Here we have 'the last word' in modern large-scale capitalist engineering and planned organisation, *subordinated to Junker-bourgeois imperialism.* Cross out the words in italics, and in place of the militarist, Junker, bourgeois, imperialist *state* put *also a state*, but of a different social type, of a different class content — a *Soviet* state, that is, a proletarian state, and you will have the *sum total* of the conditions necessary for socialism. Socialism is inconceivable without large-scale capitalist engineering based on the latest discoveries of modern science. It is inconceivable without planned state organisation, which keeps tens of millions of people to the strictest observance of a unified standard in production and distribution ... *In 1918 Germany and Russia have become the most striking embodiment of the material realisation of the economic, the productive and the socio-economic conditions for socialism, on the one hand, and the political conditions, on the other* [my emphasis, C.C-U.] ... While the revolution in Germany is still slow 'coming forth', our task is to study the state capitalism of the Germans, to spare *no effort* in copying it. Our task is to hasten this copying even more than Peter I hastened the copying of the Western culture by barbarian Russia, and we must not hesitate to use barbarous methods in fighting barbarism."[35]

The plainness with which Lenin expresses himself at the end of this passage enables us to judge the capital importance he assigns to the problem. But neither in this passage nor in any other does Lenin ask himself whether there are not *organic* links binding the existing form of industrialisation to the capitalist system of exploiting the productive forces: whether, in other words, capitalist production-relations are something more than the mere contingent form of industrialisation as it has developed up to now. At no moment do we see surfacing in Lenin's thought the idea that, although "without this basis of industrialisation there can be no question of socialism, nevertheless it only determines the 'lower limit' of socialist transformations",[36] that socialisation of the means of production may require and imply, not only from the standpoint of technical progress but also, and above all, from that of social progress a radically different sort of industrialisation. To excuse Lenin, it has been suggested that he saw in large-scale industry only the absolutely necessary point of departure for socialist construction. However, a close reading of his works shows that, for him, the point of departure tends to be identified with the point of arrival, and that this form of industrialisation appears as the infallible guarantee of the *final* victory of socialism.

> "Communism implies Soviet power as a political organ, enabling the mass of the oppressed to run all state affairs — without that, communism is unthinkable ... This guarantees political success. Economic success, however, can be assured only when the Russian proletarian state effectively controls a huge industrial machine built on up-to-date technology ..."[37]

Any doubt that may still be possible vanishes when we find Lenin tackling directly the question of productivity and of the type of social organisation of labour which is necessary in order to raise it. If, as we have seen, productivity is the touchstone of socialist construction, then what has to be done is to catch up with and surpass the advanced industrial countries, which remain the obligatory criterion. For Lenin the question of productivity is central, since it involves not only the economic development but also the cultural and social development of the new proletarian regime.

"In every socialist revolution, after the proletariat has solved the problem of capturing power ... there necessarily comes to the forefront the fundamental task of creating a social system superior to capitalism, namely, raising the productivity of labour, and in this connexion (and for this purpose) securing better organisation of labour ... The raising of the productivity of labour first of all requires that the material basis of large-scale industry shall be assured ... Another condition for raising the productivity of labour is, firstly, the raising of the educational and cultural level of the mass of the population ... Secondly, a condition for economic revival is the raising of the working people's discipline, their skill, the effectiveness, the intensity of labour and its better organisation."[38]

All the key elements of Lenin's conception are brought together in this passage, but without their real content being made explicit. It is therefore important, first and foremost, to consider what exactly Lenin meant by "a social system superior to capitalism", and by "securing better organisation of labour", and, since these are subordinated to the requirements for raising productivity, by what route "the raising of the educational level of the mass of the population" and the development of "working people's discipline" were to proceed.

Lenin takes a clear stand on all these points. There is no need to look for some original way of organising labour, because one exists which has proved its worth and only needs to be taken over — that, precisely, which has made possible the increase in productivity which socialist society must achieve. This organisation of labour is, of course, the one that capitalism created and perfected: separated from the purposes of class-exploitation which the bourgeois system has imposed upon it from without, it becomes perfectly and immediately usable, just as it stands, for realising the objectives of the revolution, and it spontaneously acquires a proletarian class character.

> *"We shall not invent the organisational form of the work, but take it ready-made from capitalism* — we shall take over the banks, syndicates, the best factories, experimental stations, academies, and so forth; all that we shall have to do is to borrow the best models furnished by the advanced countries."[39]

This type of organisation of labour, and so of social organisation, which is inseparable from it, is characterised above all by its "high degree of rationalisation", its efficient methods of administration and management of enterprises, its incentives to work, and so on. All this, let me repeat, represents for Lenin only a set of means, of mere tools, the class nature of which is defined and guaranteed elsewhere, in the *locus* where the *political form* of the government is determined. Actually, as I have tried to show at some length in the preceding chapters, in that *locus* too the means are nothing by themselves: the decisive factor is the use made of them: it is a question, in short, of "who holds power". Why, Lenin's answer comes at once, "the state is the workers, the advanced section of the workers, the vanguard. We are the state". And in this state "the power of the workers and the poor is assured".[40]

We find a concrete example which is especially illuminating in this connexion in the passages where Lenin advocates the adoption of the Taylor system, the last word in rationalisation of the labour-process on the basis of large-scale machine industry.

"We must raise the question of piece work and apply and test it in practice; we must raise the question of applying much of what is scientific and progressive in the Taylor system; we must make wages correspond to the total amount of goods turned out, or to the amount of work done by the railways, the water transport system, etc., etc. The Russian is a bad worker compared with people in advanced countries. It could not be otherwise under the Tsarist regime and in view of the persistence of the hang-over from serfdom. The task that the Soviet Government must set the people in all its scope is — learn to work. The Taylor system, the last word of capitalism in this respect, like all capitalist progress, is a combination of the refined brutality of bourgeois exploitation and a number of the greatest scientific achievements in the field of analysing mechanical motions during work, the elimination of superfluous and awkward motions, the elaboration of correct methods of work, the introduction of the best system of accounting and control, etc. The Soviet Republic must at all costs adopt all that is valuable in the achievements of science and technology in this field. The possibility of building socialism depends exactly upon our success in combining the Soviet power and the Soviet organisation of administration with the up-to-date achievements of capitalism."[41]

As may be seen, it does not occur to Lenin for one moment that the "refined brutality" of the Taylor system is not in essence due to its use by the bourgeoisie but, much more fundamentally, to its intrinsic characteristics. Lenin does not seem even to suspect that the Taylor system may be based, above all and necessarily, upon a way of producing the means of life in which the producer, the individual, is unable to recognise himself in his work or in the outcome of his work, just as the way that this work is carried on becomes completely alien to him and outside his control: that the Taylor system, in fact, *implies*, in its very efficiency and profitability, labour that is alienated labour *par excellence*, and the nature of which does not result from its being used in the capitalist mode of production, even though it arose there, but is inherent in the very type of organisation of labour that it represents.

I therefore think we are justified in concluding that, for Lenin, the "superiority" of the organisation of labour of which he speaks lies not in its nature as such, which is unchanged, but in its different political purpose, serving the proletarian state, that is, the masses. In other words, this form of organisation of labour, once assimilated by the Soviet power, immediately becomes superior because it is directed towards a new destination. It lies in the logic of this analysis that Lenin feels no need to raise, even at a theoretical level, the question of a possible contradiction in terms, and to consider the prospect of the gap that might perhaps appear, in the more or less distant future, between, on the one hand, the aim being pursued, and, on the other, certain features of the road being travelled, determined by the point of departure adopted.

When we read these theses we can easily deduce what the "new" discipline of the working people is to be. It is determined directly by large-scale industrial production, in contact with which it was forged, and from which it derives its special character and its strength. Its novelty and superiority as compared with the previous epoch results from the fact that it is, or should aim to be, the outcome of conscious action by the working people, who understand that henceforth they are working for the proletarian state, that is, for themselves, and that the interests of large-scale industry are also their interests.

> "The socialist revolution ... places firmly in the fore-front the problems of proletarian discipline and organisation of the working people and ability to tackle the work with strictly businesslike methods and knowledge of the interests of large-scale industry. These problems the proletariat must solve in practice, for otherwise it will suffer defeat."[42]

The proletariat will demonstrate its political maturity by submitting to the "iron discipline" which is indispensable for productive labour, and which is imperatively demanded by large-scale industry. This discipline pre-sumes, in its turn, a type of administration and management the most finished form of which Lenin finds in the system of one-man command in the army. The latter provides a generic model indicating the line to be followed by all social organisation of labour and production.[43]

> "In regard to ... the importance of individual dicta-torial powers from the point of view of the specific tasks of the present moment, it must be said that large-scale machine industry — which is precisely the material source, the productive source, the foundation of socialism — calls for absolute and strict *unity of will*, which directs the joint labours of hundreds, thousands and tens of thousands of people ... But how can strict unity of will be ensured? By thousands subordinating their will to the will of one ... This is the most difficult, but the most gratifying task, because only its fulfilment will give us a socialist system. We must learn to combine the public meeting' democracy of the working people — turbulent, surging, overflowing its banks like a spring flood — with iron discipline while at work, with *unquestioning obedience* to the will of a single person, the Soviet leader, while at work."[44]

Here again it never strikes Lenin that this blind activity, this absolute subordination to the will of a single person while at work — even if we assume that they are, to start with, the conscious result of a considered act — contain the danger, inherent in this type of attitude, of influencing the general behaviour of society as a whole, at every level, and thereby of simultaneously destroying with one hand what it was hoped was being built with the other. The essential thing, for Lenin, remains, above all, the establishment, at any cost, of a well-organised, productive economy, on the model of the capitalist industrial societies. But, inevitably, the "vicious circle" reappears: organisation and management of the economy on the basis of large-scale machine industry depend, as the experience of advanced societies shows, upon knowledge, and above all on scientific and technical knowledge, which cannot be either improvised or invented. They require *culture*, and cultured persons, "specialists". Well, there is no need to repeat that the proletariat and the masses in general do not answer to these requirements. And so, in order that "workers' control" (for Lenin, the first phase of socialism) may give way to workers' management (the second, "higher" phase of socialism), the proletariat is more interested than anyone else in learning from the Western industrial societies and, as a direct consequence, from the bourgeois specialists. To deny the necessity of "learning from the bourgeoisie", says Lenin, means showing that one has "the psychology of an inhabitant of Central Africa",[45] and rashly forgetting that thesis of Kautsky's which Lenin made his own: only experience enables one to know what large-scale production entails, and only "the trust organisers" can pass on this knowledge to the masses.[46]

"We shall now learn from them because we lack knowledge, because we do not have this knowledge. We know about socialism, but knowledge of organisation on a scale of millions, knowledge of the organisation and distribution of goods, etc. — this we do not have ... And we say, let him be a

thoroughgoing rascal even, but if he has organised a
trust, if he is a merchant who has dealt with the
organisation and distribution for millions and tens
of millions, if he has acquired experience — we must
learn from him."[47]

All Lenin's statements about the need for ever more
direct participation by the masses in the management of
their own affairs prove to be limited in their bearing by
the way in which he presents the problem of management
in terms of *competence*, and derives this from knowledge
and all culture in general: practice is inseparable from it,
but seems to come in only to confirm this competence, to
consolidate and "polish" it, so to speak. Thus, being
subject to the same rule here as that which governs,
according to Lenin, its acquisition of class-consciousness,
the proletariat, as a concrete class, cannot accomplish by
its own efforts alone the development of those "creative
faculties" it is supposed to bear within itself as an
historical class. And it can acquire the one like the other,
competence like consciousness, only through the trans-
mission of knowledge. Therefore, after having delegated
its powers to the Party in the sphere of political
leadership, the proletariat must do the same in that
sphere which yet affects it most immediately and
concretely — the sphere of the organisation of its own
labour, that is, the main part of its day-to-day life in
society.

" 'Management' is entrusted by the Soviet power to
capitalists not as capitalists but as technicians or
organisers, for higher salaries ... But it is precisely
these people whom we, the proletarian party, must

appoint to 'manage' the labour process and the organisation of production, for there are *no* other people who have practical experience in this matter ... Only those are worthy of the name of Communists who understand that it is *impossible* to create or introduce socialism *without learning* from the organisers of the trusts. For socialism is not a figment of the imagination, but the assimilation and application by the proletarian vanguard, which has seized power, of what has been created by the trusts. We, the party of the proletariat, have *no other way* of acquiring the ability to organise large-scale production on trust lines, as trusts are organised, except by acquiring it from first-class capitalist experts."
[48]

There can be no doubt that the road advocated by Lenin corresponded to his profound conviction that he was serving the revolution by trying to rescue it from universal chaos and re-establish a ruined economy by the only method which seemed to him to guarantee *immediate* results, and which the proletariat and the masses in general could actually and consciously accept. What weighed heavily upon the subsequent fate of the revolution was when the type of personal and collective behaviour, the mode of social conduct, dictated by a situation of necessity (that same "old filthy business" that Marx and Engels spoke of) tended to be presented as "normality", as something wholly legitimate; when the exception became the rule: when, in short, Lenin maintained that:

"there is ... absolutely *no* contradiction in principle

between Soviet (*that is*, socialist) democracy and the
exercise of dictatorial powers by the individuals",
[49]

and pointed to the lesson to be drawn from the
experience of the army in the matter of organisation:

"Developing systematically, it passed from a corporate form that was casual and vague to a corporate form elevated to the status of a system of
organisation and permeating all the institutions of
the army; and now, as a general tendency, it has
arrived at the principle of one-man responsibility
as *the only correct method of work*".[50]

Like the history of the world according to Hegel, the
factory, Lenin might have said, "is not the theatre of
happiness". But no-one *knows* this better than the
workers, since they are the ones who *experience* it in their
everyday lives. And this is precisely why Lenin's ideas
mean there is to be no change for them — for the class for
and by whom everything was to be changed. For the
factory is not merely, as Lenin seems to "forget", the
place where footwear and tractors are made, but also and
above all the place where a certain structure of social
relations between men is created and reproduced, a
structure the mechanisms of which are necessarily based
on the division of labour and, consequently, on the
division of the producers into those who direct and those
who execute, those who give orders and those who obey,
those who "know" what has to be done and those who
"wait to be told" what they have to do. The dialectic of

history is not such that blind obedience engenders a spirit of initiative, that unconditional subordination fosters a critical and personalised attitude, or that treating men as tools results in creative activity on their part. It is not possible to "disalienate" by alienating means. The fact that the man in charge is "Soviet" does not affect the essential nature of that cunning process which, as Rakovsky put it, leads from functional subordination to social subjection. And this is all the more the case if, as I have already pointed out, the mechanisms of control "from below", to which Lenin rightly ascribed such importance, become worn out through trying to control something which actually escapes by another channel from their "historical" but incompetent mandate. Here, the history of the class struggle has extensively demonstrated the dialectic of the disintegration of popular control, which is, it cannot be too much emphasised, *both cause and effect* of a situation in which the masses are more "acted upon" than "acting".

What, in Lenin's analysis, lies open to criticism is not so much that he opted for methods that gave immediate results as that he accorded these methods, for this very reason, a legitimacy which ruled out the need to keep constantly open the question of their real suitability in relation to the socialist nature of the revolutionary process, or, in other words, as I have already said, the question whether there was an inherent relationship between the type of industrialisation adopted and the capitalist nature of the system which had made it possible *that* development of the productive forces. In my opinion, such criticism is doubly valid. In the first place, the theoretical premises for *raising* the problem existed, starting with the writings of Marx and Engels themselves, for whom, "the communist materialist sees (in the situation of the working class) the necessity, and at the same time the condition, of a transformation *both* of industry and of the social structure".[51] *Capital*, too, furnishes an analysis of large-scale machine industry from which the logical conclusion to be drawn, even if this remains only implicit in the text, is that it cannot serve as it stands for the process of building a socialist society:

"The separation of the intellectual faculties of the production process from manual labour, and the transformation of those faculties into powers exercised by capital over labour, is, as we have already shown, finally completed by large-scale industry erected on the foundation of machinery. The special skill of each individual machine-operator, who has now been deprived of all significance, vanishes as an infinitesimal quantity in the face of the science, the gigantic natural forces, and the mass of social labour embodied in the system of machinery, which, together with those three forces, constitutes the power of the 'master' ... The technical subordination of the worker to the uniform motion of the instruments of labour, and the peculiar composition of the working group, consisting as it does of individuals of both sexes and all ages, gives rise to a barrack-like discipline, which is elaborated into a complete system in the factory, and brings the previously mentioned labour of superintendence to its fullest development, thereby dividing the workers into manual labourers and overseers, into the private soldiers and the N.C.O.s of an industrial army".[52]

In the second place, the problem was raised in a practical way, in the early years of Soviet Russia, within the actual leadership of the Bolshevik Party. The tendency that first expressed itself on this matter was that of the "Left Communists", whose short-lived journal *Kommunist* went straight to the heart of the problem:

"The introduction of labour discipline in connexion with the restoration of capitalist management of industry cannot substantially increase the productivity of labour, but it will diminish the class initiative, activity and organisation of the proletariat. It threatens to enslave the working class ..."

"If the proletariat itself does not know how to create the necessary prerequisite for the socialist organisation of labour, no-one can do this for it, and no-one can compel it to do this."[53]

The second noteworthy manifestation of the unease produced by the policy being followed was crystallised around the "Workers' Opposition" group, the presence in which of a large number of Bolshevik trade-union leaders, those very leaders who maintained the closest ties with the concrete reality of the masses, testifies to the importance of the questions raised and the echo they evoked among the masses. In her pamphlet written for this group, Alexandra Kollontai, one of its most outstanding representatives, repeated, while developing them, the ideas already put forward in *Kommunist*.

The "specialists", she said, constitute a

"group which is not only inherently foreign to Communism, but absolutely unable to develop the

right qualities for introducing new forms of organising the work, new motives for increasing production, new approaches to production and distribution ... The whole controversy simmers down to one
basic question: who shall build the communist
economy and how shall it be built? ... In a labour
republic the development of productive forces by
means of technique plays a secondary role in comparison with the second factor, that of the efficient
organisation of labour, and creation of a new system
of economy. Even if Soviet Russia succeeds in carrying out completely its project of general electrification, without introducing any essential change in the
system of control and organisation of the people's
economy and production, it would only catch up
with the advanced capitalist countries in the matter
of development".[54]

To both the "Left Communists" and the "Workers'
Opposition" Lenin replied by setting forth the theses I
have reproduced in these pages, and he did not give up
until they had been adopted by the Party.

In these views of Lenin's which I have tried to
present in a systematic way we find, eventually, what we
saw looming behind his conception of culture. Knowledge and Civilisation are the prerogative of industrial
society, and present themselves as a sort of purely
objective entity, something aseptic which is "already
there" and which *may*, when placed in certain historical
circumstances, bear with it certain ideological values, the
bourgeois or proletarian nature of which is not, on the
whole, inherent but added to it. These views are both
origin and result of the circumstance that Lenin does not

seem to have had even an inkling of the need to make a radical critique of industrial civilisation,

> "the *ratio* of which is clearly rooted elsewhere than in man himself, and represents *par excellence* the rationality of certain relations, or of man as the mere agent of these relations, a *ratio* that has been applied to man from without"[55]

— the need, after all, for socialism to create *its own* basis of civilisation. In other words, Lenin remains, despite himself, prisoner to that convention of the ruling ideology of advanced capitalism, born of and with industrialisation, according to which modern science and technology, together with the organisation based upon them, are "neutral", from the social and human standpoint. As I have shown in Part One (see p.37), Lenin "slips" into the (ideological) illusion of his epoch, maintained by the opacity of its social relations, for

> "never, in any earlier period, have the productive forces taken on a form so *indifferent* to the intercourse of individuals as individuals ..."[56]

As we saw at the outset, Lenin was one of the first to appreciate the original and unforeseen nature of a revolutionary situation in which the ignorant masses of a country that was barely "civilised", because barely industrialised, found themselves forced, so to speak, like the Paris Communards, to "storm heaven":

"What about a people that found itself in a revolutionary situation such as that created during the first imperialist war? Might it not, influenced by the hopelessness of its situation, fling itself into a struggle that would offer it at least some chance of securing conditions for the further development of civilisation that were somewhat unusual?"[57]

However, Lenin explains, a little later, what he means by "securing conditions ... that were somewhat unusual". All it means, at bottom, is catching up with and surpassing the Western states; in other words, attaining by the *same path* of industrialisation the degree of development of the productive forces needed in order to establish socialism completely — but doing it (and in this lies all that is "original" in the Russian Revolution) within the setting of a political regime which is already proletarian. It seems that, consequently, all Lenin's energy is concentrated in his stubborn effort to fit the Russian Revolution on to the rails of "normality", to make the replies given to the new questions posed by the revolution as a practical phenomenon coincide as closely as possible with the theoretical schema of the revolution. More profoundly still, there emerges from Lenin's thought the conviction that all that is needed, now that the political form of the ruling power is revolutionary and proletarian, even if the proletariat does exercise its dictatorship through the Party, its "authentic" representative — that all that is needed is to develop, at whatever cost, the productive forces, by means of the methods that have been tested by the advanced industrial societies. As soon as the required level has been reached, evolution towards socialism will be ineluctable, objectively inscribed in the historical process.

On the one hand, development of the productive forces (the material basis), on the other, the Party's knowledge and determination (the revolutionary plan) — these are, at bottom, what Lenin sees as the two parameters of the revolution, on which depend such variables as the maturity (consciousness) of the masses, their assimilation of (bourgeois) culture, and, thereby, their real and direct accession to power. Lenin's reply to the fundamental question that he himself raises thus comes quite "naturally":

"We gained practical experience in a matter which had never before confronted us, but without which it is impossible to achieve communism. I say again that the task of combining the victorious proletarian revolution with bourgeois culture, with bourgeois science and technology, which up to now has been available to few people, is a difficult one. *Here, everything depends on the organisation and discipline of the advanced sections of the working people*".[58]

It remains for us to consider what is the bearing of these assumptions, and the conception of the problematic of the cultural revolution which they imply, upon the proclaimed objectives of the proletarian revolution: the abolition of class society and the ending of the alienation of concrete man based on the production-relations engendered by class exploitation — objectives of which Marx and Engels repeated again and again that they would either be won by the masses themselves or not at all.

NOTES

1 Marx, *Capital*, Vol.I, London, Penguin, 1976, p.99.
2 Marx and Engels, *Werke*, Vol.30, Berlin, 1964, pp.490 and 495. [The first sentence, but not the second, of this quotation from Marx's letter to Freiligrath, 29 February 1860, is given in Marx and Engels, *Selected Correspondence*, Moscow, F.L.P.H., 1956, p.147.]
3 Marx and Engels, *The German Ideology*: in *Collected Works*, Vol.5, *op.cit.* p.87.
4 Marx and Engels, *Collected Works*, Vol.5, *op.cit.*, p.4.
5 *C.W.*, Vol.5, p.384.
6 *Ibid.*, p.422.
7 Karl Kautsky, in *Neue Zeit*, 1901-1902, XX, I, No. 3, p.79, as quoted by Lenin in *C.W.*, Vol.5, pp.383-384.
8 Marx and Engels, *Collected Works*, Vol.5, *op.cit.*, p.52 (my emphasis, C.C-U.)
9 R. Rossanda, "De Marx à Marx", in *Il Manifesto*, Paris, Le Seuil, 1971, p.290.
10 K. Papaioannou, "Classes et Parti", in *Le Contrat Social*, Vol.VII, No.4, pp.215 and 217-218: and Hegel, *The Philosophy of Right*, para.187, in *Great Books of the Western World, No. 46: Hegel, The Philosophy of Right and the Philosophy of History*, Chicago, Encyclopaedia Britannica, 1952, p.65.
11 *C.W.*, Vol. 5, pp.375-376 (my emphasis, C.C-U.).
12 Rosa Luxemburg, "Organisational Questions of Russian Social Democracy", (1904), in *Select Political Writings of Rosa Luxemburg*, ed. D. Howard, New York, Monthly Review Press, 1972, p.306.
13 *C.W.*, Vol.26, p.469: *Report on the Activities of the*

Council of People's Commissars, 11(24) January 1918: "As a democratic government, we cannot ignore the decision of the masses of the people, even though we may disagree with it ... And even if the peasants continue to follow the Socialist-Revolutionaries, even if they give this party a majority in the Constituent Assembly, we shall still say — what of it? Experience is the best teacher and it will show who is right ... Experience will oblige us to draw together in the general stream of revolutionary creative work, in the elaboration of new state forms. We must be guided by experience; we must allow complete freedom to the creative faculties of the masses" (*C.W.*, Vol.26, pp.260-261).

14 *C.W.*, Vol.26, p.297: *To The Population*, 5(18) November 1917.

15 F. Bon and M. A. Burnier, *Classe ouvrière et révolution*, Paris, Le Seuil, 1971, pp.67-68.

16 At the Tenth Congress of the Bolshevik Party, in March 1921, Lenin said: "Marxism teaches — and this tenet has not only been formally endorsed by the whole of the Communist International in the decisions of the Second (1920) Congress of the Comintern on the role of the political party of the proletariat, but has also been confirmed in practice by our revolution — that only the political party of the working class, i.e., the Communist Party, is capable of uniting, training and organising a vanguard of the proletariat and of the whole mass of the working people that alone will be capable of withstanding the inevitable petty-bourgeois vacillations of this mass and the inevitable traditions and relapses of narrow craft unionism or craft prejudices among the proletariat, and of guiding all the united activities of the whole of the proletariat, i.e., of leading it politically, and,

through it, the whole mass of the working people. Without this, the dictatorship of the proletariat is impossible" (*C.W.*, Vol.32, p.246).

17 "A beginning can and must be made at once, overnight, to replace the specific 'bossing' of state officials by the simple functions of 'foremen and accountants', functions which are already fully within the ability of the average town dweller and can well be performed for 'workmen's wages'. *We*, the workers, shall organise large-scale production on the basis of what capitalism has already created, relying on our own experience as workers, establishing strict, iron discipline backed up by the state power of the armed workers. We shall reduce the role of state officials to that of simply carrying out our instructions as responsible, revocable, modestly paid 'foremen and accountants' (of course, with the aid of technicians of all sorts, types and degrees). *This* is *our* proletarian task, this is what we can and must *start* with in accomplishing the proletarian revolution. Such a beginning, on the basis of large-scale production, will of itself lead to the gradual 'withering-away' of all bureaucracy, to the gradual creation of an order — an order without inverted commas, an order bearing no similarity to wage-slavery — an order under which the functions of control and accounting, becoming more and more simplle, will be performed by each in turn, will then become a habit and will finally die out as the *special* function of a special section of the population" (*C.W.*, Vol.25, p.426).

18 *C.W.*, Vol.33, p.488: (*Better Fewer, But Better*, 2 March 1923.)

19 *C.W.*, Vol.32, p.21: *The Trade Unions, The Present Situation and Trotsky's Mistakes*, 30 December 1920: my emphasis, C.C-U. It was also in connexion with

the trade unions that Lenin wrote, for example: "The trade unions must collaborate closely and constantly with the government, all the political and economic activities of which are guided by the class-conscious vanguard of the working class — the Communist Party" (*C.W.*, Vol.33, p.190).

20 *C.W.*, Vol.26, pp.105-106: *Can the Bolsheviks retain state power?*, end of September — 1(14) October 1917. [The published translation is unfortunate: for "mutilates" read "disfigures": *Trans.*]

21 "We have learned something, and in order to march ahead and to overcome economic chaos what we have to do is not to start anew, not to reconstruct everything right and left, but to *utilise* to the utmost what has already been created. There must be as little general reconstruction as possible and as many as possible business-like measures, ways, means and directions for the attainment of our chief aim which have been tested in practice and verified by results — we must have more workers in our apparatus, and see that it is done still more widely, still more rapidly, and still better, we must enlist an even greater number of workers and labouring peasants in the work of administering industry and the national economy generally ..." (*C.W.*, Vol.30, pp.405-406).

22 "*All administrative work requires special qualifications.* You may be the very best of revolutionaries and propagandists, and yet be absolutely useless as an administrator. But anybody who studies real life and has practical experience knows that management necessarily implies competence, that a knowledge of all the conditions of production down to the last detail and of the latest technology of your branch of production is required; you must have had a certain scientific training" (*C.W.*, Vol.30, p.428: my

emphasis, C.C-U.)

23 *C.W.*, Vol.33, p.252, Or, again: "*We have sufficient, quite sufficient political power*; we also have sufficient economic resources at our command, but the vanguard of the working class which has been brought to the forefront to directly supervise, to determine the boundaries, to demarcate, to subordinate and not be subordinated itself, lacks sufficient *ability* for it. All that is needed here is ability, and that is what we do not have" (*C.W.*, Vol.33, p.279, my emphasis, C.C-U.).

24 *C.W.*, Vol.36, p.521: *Speech at a meeting of the Communist group in the All-Russia Central Executive Committee of the Trade Unions*, 15 March 1920: my emphasis, C.C-U.

25 *C.W.*, Vol.36, p.588: *Outline of a speech, not actually delivered, to the 10th All-Russia Congress of Soviets*, December 1922.

26 *C.W.*, Vol.33, pp.287-289: *Political Report to the 11th Party Congress*, 27 March 1922: my emphasis, C.C-U. In another passage Lenin repeats the same idea, using to illustrate it an image that is certainly striking: "Communists, revolutionaries who have accomplished the greatest revolution in the world, on whom the eyes of, if not forty centuries, from the height of the pyramids, then, at all events, forty European countries are turned in the hope of emancipation from capitalism, must learn from ordinary salesmen. But these ordinary salesmen have had ten years' warehouse experience and know the business, whereas the responsible Communists and devoted revolutionaries do not know the business, and do not even realise that they do not know it" (*C.W.*, Vol.33, pp.275-276).

27 As far back as 1904 Trotsky had prophesied this

process of "substitution", of which he was to be later one of the first victims. The Party would tend, he said, to substitute itself for the class, then the Central Committee for the Party, and, eventually, the leader would substitute himself for the Central Committee. (*Nashi politicheskie zadachi*, Geneva, 1904, p.54: French translation, *Nos Tâches Politiques*, Paris, Belfond, 1970, p.128.)

28 *C.W.*, Vol.36, p.573: *Notes for a speech*, 27 March 1922. Again: "All of us are sunk in the rotten bureaucratic swamp of 'departments'. Great authority, common sense and strong will are necessary for the everyday struggle against this. The departments are shit; decrees are shit. To find men and check up on their work — that is the whole point" (*C.W.*, Vol.36, p.566).

29 *C.W.*, Vol.33, p.257: *On the conditions for admitting new members to the Party*, 26 March 1922: my emphasis, C.C-U.

30 Rakovsky, letter to Valentinov, quoted by Trotsky in *The Revolution Betrayed*, London, New Park Publications, 1973, p.102.

31 Marx and Engels, *The German Ideology*, in *Collected Works*, Vol.5, *op.cit.*, p.49.

32 Trotsky, *Terrorism and Communism*, University of Michigan Press, Ann Arbor Paperback, 1961, p.145.

33 *C.W.*, Vol.27, p.212: *Original version of the article "The Immediate Tasks of the Soviet Government"*, 29 March 1918.

34 *C.W.*, Vol.30, p.313: *Speech at the 3rd All-Russia Congress of Economic Councils*, 27 January 1920: my emphasis, C.C-U.

35 *C.W.*, Vol.27, pp.339-340: *'Left-Wing' Childishness and the Petty-Bourgeois Mentality*, 5 May 1918.

36 R. Richta, *La Civilisation au carrefour*, Paris,

Anthropos, 1972, p.34, n.32.

37 *C.W.*, Vol.31, p.420: *Our Foreign and Domestic Position and the Tasks of the Party*, 21 Nov. 1920.

38 *C.W.*, Vol.27, pp.257-258: *The Immediate Tasks of the Soviet Government*, March-April 1918.

39 *C.W.*, Vol.26, p.110: *Can the Bolsheviks retain state power?* End of September-1 (14) October 1917: my emphasis, C.C-U.

40 *C.W.*, Vol.33, p.278: *Speech at the 11th Party Congress*, 27 March 1922 and Vol.27, p.339: *'Left-Wing' Childishness and the Petty-Bourgeois Mentality*, 5 May 1918.

41 *C.W.*, Vol.27, pp.258-259: *The Immediate Tasks of the Soviet Government*, March-April 1918. Trotsky, too, adopted this thesis, as a result of the same line of reasoning: "Under capitalism, the system of piece-work and of grading, the application of the Taylor system, etc., have as their object to increase the exploitation of the workers by the squeezing-out of surplus-value. Under Socialist production, piece-work, bonuses, etc., have as their problem [i.e. task — *Trans.*] to increase the volume of social product, and consequently to raise the general well-being" (*Terrorism and Communism, op.cit.*, p.149).

42 *C.W.*, Vol.27, p.287: *Session of the All-Russia Central Executive Committee*, 29 April 1918.

43 "The experience of the Soviet government in army organisation must not be regarded as something isolated. War embraces all forms of organisation in all spheres ... This experience is worth thinking about ... At best, corporate management involves a tremendous waste of forces and is not suited to the rapid and accurate work demanded by the conditions of centralised large-scale industry" (*C.W.*, Vol.30, pp.309-310: *Speech at the 3rd Congress of Economic*

Councils, 27 January 1920).

44 *C.W.*, Vol.27, pp.268-269 and 271: *The Immediate Tasks of the Soviet Government*, March-April 1918.

45 *C.W.*, Vol.27, p.310: *Session of the All-Russia Central Executive Committee*, 29 April 1918.

46 "I will remind you from Kautsky's authoritative pamphlet how he conceived life the day after the social revolution. I will tell you approximately what he wrote: the trust organisers will not be left without work to do" (*C.W.*, Vol.27, p.313).

47 *C.W.*, Vol.27, pp.296-297: *Session of the All-Russia Central Executive Committee*, 29 April 1918.

48 *C.W.*, Vol.27, pp.349-350: *Left-Wing Childishness and the Petty-Bourgeois Mentality*, 5 May 1918.

49 *C.W.*, Vol.27, p.268: *The Immediate Tasks of the Soviet Government*, March-April, 1918.

50 *C.W.*, Vol.30, p.310: *Speech at the 3rd Congress of Economic Councils*, 27 January 1920: my emphasis, C.C-U. It is important to stress that Lenin does not confine these views on one-man management versus "corporate" management to the economic sphere of the production process, but extends them also to the *political* sphere. An eloquent example is provided by his analysis of the reasons why the Treaty of Brest-Litovsk had to be signed: "The Treaty of Brest-Litovsk was forced upon us because we were helpless in every way. *What sort of period was it? It was a period of impotence*, from which we emerged victorious. *It was a period in which corporate management was universal*" (*C.W.*, Vol.30, p.459: *Report of the Central Committee to the 9th Party Congress*, 29 March 1920: my emphasis, C.C-U.).

51 Marx and Engels, *The German Ideology*, in *Collected Works*, Vol.5, *op.cit.*, p.41. My emphasis, C.C-U.

52 *Capital*, Vol.I, London, Penguin, 1976, pp.548-549.

53 *Kommunist*, published by the Moscow Regional Bureau of the Bolshevik Party, No. 1, 20 April, 1918, p.8, and No. 2, 27 April 1918, p.6.

54 A. Kollontai, *The Workers' Opposition* (1921) re-issued as Solidarity Pamphlet No. 7, Reading, no date: pp.9, 16, 27-28.

55 R. Richta, *La Civilisation au carrefour*, *op.cit.*, pp.85-86.

56 Marx and Engels, *The German Ideology*, in *Collected Works*, Vol.5, *op.cit.*, pp.86-87, my emphasis, C.C-U.

57 *C.W.*, Vol.33, p.478: *Our Revolution*, 16 January 1923.

58 *C.W.*, Vol.29, p.74: *The Achievements and Difficulties of the Soviet Government*, March-April 1919: my emphasis, C.C-U.

Conclusions

"In reality and for the practical materialist, i.e., the Communist, it is a question of revolutionising the existing world, of practically coming to grips with and changing the things found in existence."[1] As I pointed out at the beginning of this analysis, the "revolutionising" — this term has the advantage over "revolution" that it takes better account of the *temporal* dimension of the revolutionary process — must necessarily, if it is to satisfy its own purposes, be radical and total (or, more precisely still, totalising): it must go to the root of all social relations, all social structures, in their totality. The conditions for this revolutionising are a certain material basis (highly developed productive forces) and the taking of political power by the proletariat (manifesting a certain degree of maturity in the development of consciousness by the exploited masses). But these conditions, *sine qua non*, are no more than that, namely, the conditions for the "revolutionising" to be *possible*. As Marx says in *The Jewish Question*, political emancipation is not to be confused with human (social) emancipation: the former is "dissolved" in the latter, which transcends it.

"Only when man has recognised and organised his '*forces propres*' (own powers) as social forces, and consequently no longer separates social power from himself in the shape of *political* power, only then will human emancipation have been accomplished."[2]

The political form — in the given case, the Soviet form — of the regime which claims to be revolutionary is to be judged by the type of social (human) organisation of labour, and, consequently, of life, which underlies it and which it is assumed to express.

Similarly, the development of the productive forces and increased productivity have meaning where the interests of the revolution are concerned only insofar as the nature of the social relations based on the exploitation of the productive forces corresponds to these interests.

> "The proletarians cannot become masters of the productive forces of society except by abolishing their own previous mode of appropriation, and thereby also every other previous mode of appropriation."[3]

In the end, everything depends on the real relations, on the human quality of the relations which, in the new society (*already* new because the taking of political power is not a mere "accident" of history), men actually form among themselves and with the product of their activity, both individual and collective.

What I have tried to show is how these two conditions for the revolution's possibility "move", in Lenin's analysis, when, first, he presents them as being identical with the two parameters examined in the preceding chapters (development of the productive forces in accordance with the model furnished by the advanced capitalist societies, and proletarian political power delegated to the Party) and, secondly, he assumes that the realisation of these two parameters is necessary and sufficient to ensure the final victory of socialism. Thereby, Lenin's conceptions helped to bring about an evolution of the movement born of October the consequences of which, totally alien to the aims pursued, Lenin became aware of too late.

This evolution was none other than the process of "distortion", mentioned in the introduction, during which Soviet power was emptied of its initial revolutionary content. After making my analysis, it seems to me that we cannot understand and explain this phenomenon if we see it as merely a product of the period *after* Lenin. It seems to me, on the contrary, to be the fruit of the ripening, on both the theoretical and the practical plane, of germs which from the first years of the Russian revolution had co-existed with others, imbricated with them, to the detriment of which they had developed and which they eventually killed.

Among the many implications of these parameters we need specially to consider what becomes of culture and what it presupposes in the social (human) world to which it belongs, what it claims to express and what it really does express. It is possible, on the basis of Lenin's conception of the type of industrial society needed for the building of socialism, to see in the material infrastructure, identified with the high level of development of the productive forces, the decisive criterion for measuring the socialist quality of social progress. In order to proceed from that idea to ascribing to the development of the productive forces a value *in itself*, all that was needed was one step, which was finally taken in the so-called Stalin period and which led to a fetishising of the productive forces, from which Lenin's own attitude, as we have seen, was not exempt. This fetishising made it possible, among other things, to endow the development of the productive forces with a higher "reason of state", or even, quite

simply, to treat it as *the* "Reason of State". The growth of
the productive forces becomes the social panacea which,
until the time arrives when it has cured all ills, serves to
justify them. This was also what enabled Stalin in 1936 to
decree that socialism had been established, to repeat this
decree from time to time, and to be followed in so doing
by other "leaders of the people".[4]

Such an "economistic" determinism could not fail to
circumscribe a whole, defined cultural world, *a productionist* world regulating the relations among individuals,
between them and "their" state, even ethical and
aesthetic values, and organising "socialist society on the
lines of a huge industrial enterprise."[5] Production
becomes the point of anchorage, the compulsory
reference-point for all social values, which thereby are
deprived of all intrinsic significance and quality. They
are valuable *for* production, *in relation to* production,
and they can therefore be varied in the same way as the
requirements of this production. They are, in short,
brought down to the level of mere tools, of which it is well
known that the basic property is to "serve" and not to
raise problems. Art, science, morality, individual and
collective relations possess meaning only through and for
the sake of their utility, and contribute to the common
"well-being" only if they fit the formula which, in the last
analysis, describes the social world based on the type of
organisation of production here taken as a model:
"Work, Family, Fatherland".[6] And, under these
conditions, with the organisation of production assumed
a priori to be socialist, Soviet culture as a whole is
presented *ipso facto* as the greatest and most "human" in
the world.

It seems, in the end, that the essence of this
productionist world of culture and social relations lies in
the *absolute exteriority* of its twofold determination, the

second point of anchorage being the Party. All that was needed was to stretch a little Lenin's thesis according to which socialist consciousness can come to the masses only from without, in order that, very soon, exteriority, "legitimised" in this way, came to be fixed, or more precisely, congealed, in the Party — omniscient and thereby omnipotent. No less heavily, doubtless, than his ideas on the model to be copied as regards the type of production needed, Lenin's conception of the Party told upon the evolution of this "enlightened" vanguard of the working class, and, consequently, on the fate of the revolution — giving it a direction which he would certainly have been the first to denounce.

The pillar without which "socialist" society would go to rack and ruin, the Party is presented as being both the sacred receptacle and the refined image of the union of popular wisdom with the scientific character of "Marxist" doctrine. What the Party says is the Word of the revolution, and the "Party line" is the frontier — mobile but always right — separating into watertight compartments Good and Evil, Beauty and Ugliness, Justice and Injustice, Truth and Lies, and, to adopt a terminology which owes more to Stalin than to Plato, the Positive and the Negative. "Party spirit" (*partiinost*) becomes the fundamental value of a culture, "democratic" because "comprehensible" to the masses, in which pre-arranged questions lead to hackneyed, familiar answers, in which, as the Yugoslav philosopher S. Stojanović puts it, "the truth of authority replaces the authority of truth".[7] Consequently, the "new man" of Soviet ("socialist") reality can only be the Communist, that is, only the Party member. In him the masses can contemplate today a pre-figuration of the total man of their future. It is enough, in order to grasp what is meant, to re-read Stalin's speech after the death of Lenin — the most definitive burial that he could have been given:

> "Comrades, we Communists are people of a special mould. We are made of a special stuff ... There is nothing higher than the title of member of the Party whose founder and leader was Comrade Lenin. It is not given to everyone to be a member of such a party."[8]

It is upon this duality of the external governing factors, production and the Party, that is actually based the subtle interplay of the two types of "pull" that govern social relations in this society born of the revolution — on the one hand determinism, and, on the other, voluntarism. In their apparent mutual exclusion lies, in fact, the biggest trump held by the State, the "trick" that enables it to explain the inexplicable, to abolish real contradictions by denying them, or, what comes to the same thing, by justifying them with a dialectic no less impenetrable than the divine mysteries. This it is that makes it possible to explain, among other things, the flagrant refutations by real life of the mythical picture of life given in official accounts that are based upon "emptying out everyday, concrete reality by means of the invocation of a future guaranteed by the direction history is following".[9] One of the characters in *Cancer Ward* takes us to the heart of this complex dialectic, as applied to literature:

> "Describing something that exists is much easier than describing something that doesn't exist, even

though you know it's going to exist. What we see today with the unaided human eye is not necessarily the truth. The truth is what we *must* be, what is going to happen tomorrow. Our wonderful 'tomorrow' is what writers ought to be describing today."[10]

It is this dialectic *sui generis* which has also made it possible (and is still doing so) to "explain" the twists and turns of Soviet history by an "aberration" conveniently called "Stalinism", or "the cult of personality", and which is presented as a mere excrescence, irrational and pernicious, on a body which is healthy and immunised against all attacks other than those expressly authorised by the Party. In my view, Althusser allows himself to be taken in by this same dialectical refinement when he allows to the superstructure "a 'relative autonomy' which explains *very simply* [my emphasis, C.C-U], in theory, how the socialist *infrastructure* has been able to develop without essential damage during this period of errors affecting the superstructure".[11] Despite its "simplicity", this "explanation" remains none the less unacceptable if it claims to apply to a reality for which *socialist basic relations* are assumed. From a Marxist standpoint this line of argument is hard to defend, both practically and theoretically, since it forgets, rather conveniently, that the *locus par excellence* where the law of the relative autonomy of the superstructure operates, and must necessarily operate, in the sense of a disparity between it and its infrastructure, is none other than class society. In that society this relative autonomy means, concretely, that capitalist production-relations are compatible equally with bourgeois parliamentary democracy and with fascist dictatorship. Socialist society under construction, however, must be characterised precisely by the most thorough equivalence, or, putting it another way, the smallest gap possible, between superstructure and infrastructure, since otherwise the mystificatory opacity of class relations (distortion of concrete reality in the way that the system thinks about this reality, and causes it to be thought about) cannot give place to that social transparency to which, according to Marx, every proletarian revolution must lead.

> "The religious reflections of the real world can, in any case, vanish only when the practical relations of everyday life between man and man, and man and nature, generally present themselves to him in a transparent and rational form. The veil is not removed from the countenance of the social life-process, i.e., the process of material production, until it becomes production by freely associated men, and stands under their conscious and planned control."[12]

Thus, the infrastructure is not socialist unless the working people are effectively masters of the means of production. This necessarily implies as a condition *sine qua non*, the broadest *real* democracy in all institutions, (Party, State, etc.). On this foundation, "relative autonomy" is only the expression of the varied forms that this democracy can assume. Otherwise it would be hard to see, from a Marxist standpoint, how this autonomy could transform itself all of a sudden into something different from what it has been for centuries — the effective instrument of that mystic "veil" which it is the task of the revolution to tear away. The fact that this argument can be put forward is, in my view, a sign of something quite different from what it tries to justify. Indeed, though Althusser's "explanation" is not valid for what it seeks to explain, it contributes, unbeknown to him, to suggesting, *a contrario*, a hypothesis which Althusser obviously does not want to consider: if these "mistakes" — the gravity of which, as regards the socialist content, he himself is forced to admit, in his *Reply to John Lewis*[13] — did not affect the infrastructure of the Soviet system "in its essentials", during what is called the Stalin period and subsequently, this is perhaps just because these "essentials" already bore no resemblance in reality to the purified image of them which the superstructures tried, and still tries, to present. This hypothesis, to be sure, still has to be established, and demands, for itself alone, a whole separate study which cannot be attempted here: but one cannot, all the same, reject it out of hand in the way that, implicitly, Althusser does. For if it is possible to explain such "mistakes" on the part of the Soviet system by the relative autonomy of its superstructure, this would rather signify, it seems to me, that the basis of that superstructure, namely, the *real* production-relations, is not what the superstructure alleges. In other words, so as to "save" the socialist character of the Soviet system, Althusser finds himself obliged to have recourse to a theoretical explanation which is as reassuring as it is "simple", but which it is difficult to apply, in the measure defined, to a socialist society. In short, whatever his intention may have been, Althusser actually provides theoretical "credentials", to use his own expression, for the official "explanation" given by the ruling doctrine (which is obviously interested in describing as "mistakes" the gaps that appear between superstructure and infrastructure), and thereby lays himself open to Marx's caustic observations on the German ideologues:

"Whilst in ordinary life every shopkeeper is very well able to distinguish between what somebody professes to be and what he really is, our historiography has not yet won this trivial insight. It takes every epoch at its word and believes that everything it says and imagines about itself is true".[14]

The illusions, deliberate or unconscious, are inevitably accompanied by a sacralisation of political pronouncements in which, as Marcuse puts it, "the ritualised concept is made immune against contradictions".[15] The prime *raison d'être* of this is to give credit to the legal fiction according to which Soviet society is self-transparent, with all contradictions resolved, the concrete individual enabled to flourish, and personal and general interests reconciled. Its function, in fact, is to back up a juridical theme the ˉrequirements of which Engels summarised perfectly:

"In a modern state, law must not only correspond to the general economic condition and be its expression, but must also be an *internally coherent* expression which does not, owing to inner contradictions, reduce itself to nought. And in order to achieve this, the faithful reflection of economic conditions suffers increasingly".[16]

This sacralisation of political pronouncements is really only the "talkative" side of a false consciousness, the dark, silent side of which appears in its failure to correspond to the actual form of the production-relations and social relations that it claims to express. The more the social contradictions intensify, the more the ruling Soviet ideology, like the bourgeois ideology that Marx and Engels belaboured, descends:

> "to the level of mere idealising phrases, conscious illusion, deliberate hypocrisy. But the more their falsity is exposed by life, and the less meaning they have for consciousness itself, the more resolutely are they asserted, the more hypocritical, moral and holy becomes the language of this normal society".[17]

To this ideology, no less alienating than alienated, corresponds, point by point, the mystificatory myth of the new Soviet man, the "positive hero", champion of established values, that haunts all the dominant culture of the U.S.S.R., the unavowed nature of which consists, above all, in ensuring the reproduction of "salaried workers docile to official thinking" and "those who humbug the people"[18] — whose historical existence is as ancient as the class struggle itself.

Lenin, it must again be emphasised, would certainly not have approved of the fate that his own ideas were to experience, or of the reality that they were to serve (and still serve) to cover up and legitimise. He would probably not recognise in the hieratic figure of the new "socialist" man of official liturgical pronouncements any kinship with his own conception of the new men. That, moreover, was expressed by him more negatively than positively, but the essence of it is present in the idea that the "new man" does not exist, *and cannot exist yet*, that the germs of this development are still too weak in face of the pressure of "the old":

"The workers were never separated by a Great Wall of China from the old society. And they have preserved a good deal of the traditional mentality olf capitalist society. The workers are building a new society without themselves having become new people, or cleansed of the filth of the old world; they are still standing up to their knees in that filth. We can only dream of clearing the filth away. It would be utterly utopian to think this could be done all at once. It would be so utopian that in practice it would only postpone socialism to kingdom come". [19]

But Lenin was mistaken, for Stalin's genius made "real" that which was "utterly utopian", and caused "kingdom come" to arrive in the year 1936 — something that no Soviet leader has ever called in question. When we say that there is a connexion between these two positions, Lenin's and Stalin's, this is meant *solely* in the sense that each is one of the two possible end-results (with, in Stalin's version, caricatural and sectarian exaggeration) of one and the same conception — at bottom "mechanical", non-dialectical — of the problematic of the transformation of concrete individuals. The logic of this conception runs like this: *either* the transformation is held to be unrealisable so long as the material conditions have not been fulfilled, and then it appears as a sort of cumulative process, or the material conditions are assumed to be sufficient for this transformation to be proclaimed as *completely* realised. In the first case, that of Lenin, the transformation of the individual is postponed to future generations (whence the importance Lenin ascribed to the young people growing up after the revolution, and especially the Young Communists, who prefigured the new men of the future); in the second, that of present-day Soviet reality, this transformation is inevitably identified with a sort of pre-fabricated creature, made to measure, monolithic and optimistic. Both conceptions imply, moreover, an entity of a higher order which regulates the moments of transformation and decides the criteria whereby it is to be judged. This entity can, by definition, be nothing other than the *locus* of embodied exteriority: the Party, the Party-State, educator of the people. The circle has been squared, and the fundamental question is still being dodged, namely: who is to educate the educator? We find ourselves again at the heart of the Hegelian problematic referred to above, in the face of which one remains disarmed until the dynamic of the Marxian conception, completely "forgotten", is restored: men are never mere products of circumstances or *vice versa*, but both men and circumstances are the complex product of their reciprocal, dialectical action. The freedom of the concrete individual is the movement for his liberation. His transformation into a "new man" will never be an accomplished fact, only a fact in process of accomplishment. This is what Marx reminded Stirner of: "In revolutionary activity the changing of oneself coincides with the changing of circumstances".[20] Similarly, socialism is not "realised" after the taking of power, but its realisation nevertheless begins *from the start*, at the very moment of this event, which must *necessarily* begin the process of creating a social life and a mode of appropriating the productive forces which are *qualitatively* different. I think, let me say again, that the evolution which has led to the Soviet reality of today was not ineluctably "written" in the first phase of the Russian Revolution. We need to go back "to the sources", to try and discern, at least within the limits of the theme of the cultural revolution, some of the essential factors that determined the taking of *this* road rather than another, the possibility of which was shown by the ebullient, and therefore contradictory, life of the 1920s. While it is not a matter of presenting that period as the Golden Age preceding the "descent into hell", it is nevertheless true that, for the men of the October Revolution, the question of the quality of life, in a socialist perspective, was a problematic that they experienced and treated as something for day-to-day consideration, and with which the issue of culture was indissolubly bound up.

I have tried to show how Lenin's conception of culture, its relation to the revolution, and the assumptions underlying it — Lenin's conception of the cultural revolution, in fact — contributed to a process the result of which ended by turning against the masses whom Lenin thought he was serving in this way. The fact of their being a mere receptacle for knowledge that the masses cannot effectively dominate, and which thereby empties itself of any content relevant to the real life of these masses, engenders and develops in them a mode of behaviour, individual and collective, the characteristics of which are no longer creativity, critical spirit, initiative, combativity, sociability, and so on, but, contrariwise, conformism, passivity, indifference, individualism, and so on ... The end-result is to create and maintain, where the interests of the revolution are concerned, the demoralised, and therefore demobilising condition which Marx described in connexion with the effects of the Prussian censorship:

"It is the *censored press* that has a demoralising effect. Inseparable from it is the most powerful vice, hypocrisy, and from this, its basic vice, come all the other defects, which lack even the rudiments of virtue, and its vice of passivity, loathsome even from the aesthetic point of view. The government hears only *its own voice*, it knows that it hears only its own voice, yet it harbours the illusion that it hears the voice of the people, and it demands that the people, too, should harbour this illusion. For its part, therefore, the people sinks partly into political superstition, partly into political disbelief, or, completely turning away from political life, becomes a *rabble of private individuals*".[21]

If the ending of the social (human) alienation engendered by class society, based on the exploitation of man by man, must require "the *positive* disappearance of private property", what is then in question is the "positiveness" of this disappearance, the only true criterion of which is, consequently, the positiveness, that is, the effectiveness of the collective appropriation of the means of production. It is not enough to believe what is said in the official pronouncements, by the superstructure, through all its institutions, beginning with the Party. The "religious reflex of the real world" never recognises itself, or presents itself, as such. So long as this positiveness has not been realised in actuality, at the root of social relations, the revolution still remains to be accomplished.

NOTES

1 Marx and Engels, *The German Ideology*, in *Collected Works*, Vol.5, *op.cit.*, pp.38-39.
2 Marx, *On the Jewish Question*, in *Collected Works*, Vol.3, London, Lawrence and Wishart, 1975, p.168.

3 Marx and Engels, *Manifesto of the Communist Party*, in *Selected Works in Three Volumes*, Vol.I, *op.cit.*, p.118

4 Thus, in his report on the activity of the Central Committee of the Soviet Communist Party to the 24th Party Congress, L. Brezhnev declared: "In our country, it will be recalled, socialism triumphed back in the latter half of the thirties. This was followed by more than three decades of the Soviet people's heroic labour and struggle. Our economy of that time and our present-day economy are based on the same type of relations of production, on the same economic laws, the laws of Socialism." (*Report of the C.P.S.U. Central Committee to the 24th Congress*, 30 March 1971, Moscow, Novosti, 1971, p.46.)

5 R. Richta, *La Civilisation au carrefour*, *op.cit.*, p.293.

6 [*Travail, Famille, Patrie* was the official motto of the Vichy regime in France in 1940-1944, under Marshal Pétain — *Trans.*]

7 S. Stojanović, *Between Ideals and Reality*, New York, O.U.P., 1973, p.87.

8 Stalin, speech at the session of the 2nd All-Union Congress of Soviets devoted to Lenin's memory, 26 January 1924: *Works* (English edition), Vol.6, p.47.

9 P. Cardan, "Marxisme et théorie révolutionnaire", in *Socialisme ou Barbarie*, No. 38, X-XII, 1964, p.51.

10 A. Solzhenitsyn, *Cancer Ward*, Part I, London, Bodley Head, 1968, p.337.

11 L. Althusser, *For Marx*, *op.cit.*, p.240.

12 Marx, *Capital*, Vol.I, *op.cit.*, p.173.

13 Included in his *Essays in Self-criticism*, London; New Left Books, 1976. In this work Althusser goes somewhat further than the ideas set out in *For Marx*. He speaks of an "internal contradiction" which is to be

sought elsewhere than at the level of the super-structure alone. Nevertheless, in my view, the implicit conclusions that emerge do not basically challenge the theses of *For Marx*. He puts forward an hypothesis, at his "personal risk", he says (as though it were a quite new proposition, never uttered or analysed by other Marxist thinkers), to the effect that the phenomenon called "the cult of personality" ought more correctly to be described as a "deviation" which, in "special, converted" forms, consists in the resurgence in the working-class movement of the fundamental tendency of the Second International, namely, economism. And this deviation was not liqui-dated, as it should have been after the 20th Congress of the C.P.S.U.

It is certainly true that that Congress, by denounc-ing "Stalin's" crimes, fostered as many illusions as it destroyed, through reducing these facts to a simple "violation of socialist legality". It seems to me, though, that the concept of "deviation" inevitably presumes the existence of a point of reference which did not "deviate", and in the context this can only mean the real production-relations and social rela-tions. But it is precisely determining the nature — socialist or not socialist: and in the latter case this does not mean, I think, *a contrario*, capitalist — of this point of reference that is the essential problem. From Althusser's essay it is clear that, for him, Soviet reality is indeed socialist, so that he can properly speak of a "deviation", along with "a single socialist state" (p.89). Similarly, he never considers, even as an hypothesis no less bold than the one already made, the possibility that the class struggle in the Soviet Union may be developing in a setting which is other than socialist.

The second important feature that emerges from this analysis is the *total* absence of any critical reflexion, even in sketchy form, on the role that Lenin's thought may have played in the history of this phenomenon that Althusser proposes should be called a "deviation". If we take this silence of his at its face value, the "posthumous revenge" of the Second International must have "passed over" the Lenin period (cleansed of any hint of economism) to strike root in the Stalinist soil — the availability of which for this to happen appears a circumstance totally cut off from its immediate past.

14 Marx and Engels, *The German Ideology*, in *Collected Works*, Vol.5, *op.cit.* p.62.

15 H. Marcuse, *One-Dimensional Man*, London, Routledge, 1964, p.88.

16 Engels, letter to Conrad Schmidt, 27 October 1890, in Marx and Engels, *Selected Works in Three Volumes*, *op.cit.* Vol.3, p.492.

17 Marx and Engels, *The German Ideology*, in *Collected Works*, Vol.5, *op.cit.* p.293.

18 Che Guevara, "Socialism and Man in Cuba", in *Other Works*, London, Stage One, 1968, p.18: Gracchus Babeuf, letter to Coupé, 20 August 1791, in *Textes choisis*, Paris, Editions Sociales, 1951, p.58.

19 *C.W.*, Vol.28, pp.424-425: *Report to the 2nd All-Russia Congress of Trade Unions*, 20 January 1919.

20 Marx and Engels, *The German Ideology*, in *Collected Works*, Vol.5, *op.cit.*, p.214.

21 Marx, *Debates on Freedom of the Press, Rheinische Zeitung*, 5-19 May 1842, in Marx and Engels, *Collected Works*, Vol.I, London, Lawrence and Wishart, 1975, pp.167-168.

General Index *

*Excluding Lenin's name which, naturally, appears throughout the text.